A Roman Map

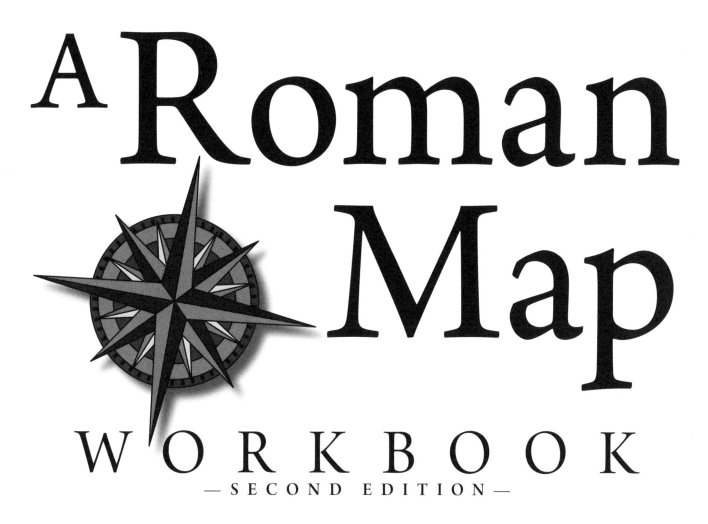

WORKBOOK
—SECOND EDITION—

By

Elizabeth Heimbach

Bolchazy-Carducci Publishers, Inc.
Mundelein, Illinois USA

Editor: Donald E. Sprague
Design & Layout: Adam Phillip Velez
Cartography: Mapping Specialists

A Roman Map Workbook
Second Edition

Elizabeth Heimbach

Bolchazy-Carducci Publishers, Inc.
1570 Baskin Road
Mundelein, Illinois 60060
www.bolchazy.com

Printed in the United States of America
2018
by Kingery Printing Company

ISBN 978-0-86516-799-5

Table of Contents

List of Maps

Preface

I started writing this map workbook more than thirty years ago when I was a young teacher struggling to hold the attention of a group of lively eighth graders whose Latin class met every day right after lunch. Geography, I found, fascinated them, and *mīrābile dictū*, they could speak in Latin about the places they located on a map of the ancient world in their textbook. That was a wonderful discovery, and led to some really worthwhile oral class activities. The students loved learning the Latin names for places they recognized in Italy and around the Mediterranean. They loved asking and answering questions in Latin about the map. I was surprised, however, to find that many of these bright students did not know which direction was east. They did not know where modern Turkey was, and they had certainly never heard of Bithynia. It was for them that I began to prepare the materials that became the first three chapters of this workbook, Ancient Italy, the World of Rome, and Roman Roads.

In other years in other schools I found the same interest in maps and the same lack of background knowledge of geography. The workbook chapter on ancient Gaul, for example, grew out of my experience with a Latin II class, a group of students who loved Caesar. They really wanted to know where the Venetī lived and whether Alesia still stood. They were studying the First World War in a history class so they were also interested to learn the ancient names for the Marne and the Seine. The next year, I wrote the Pompeii chapter for those same students when they were translating Pliny in Latin III. The materials on the city of Rome were part of their Latin III work with Cicero, while the history chapter and the materials on Greece accompanied a different class in ancient history.

I am thus enormously grateful to all of my students through all the years who loved maps and wanted to know more about the world of ancient Rome. I am also very grateful to Marie Carducci and Lou Bolchazy, who were interested in publishing a workbook with maps and exercises. They suggested the chapter on later writers of Latin, and they inspired and guided the organization of the whole workbook. Donald Sprague has been an editor extraordinaire, dealing patiently with macra and my mistakes, both large and small. Finally, I am indebted to my husband and daughters who have been enthusiastic supporters of the project.

Elizabeth Heimbach
Port Royal, Virginia

Introduction

The Latin word for map is *charta*, and this little book of *chartae* is designed to help you find your way around the world of ancient Rome. There are maps of Italy, the Mediterranean, the city of Rome and the town of Pompeii as well as maps that focus on Roman history and Roman authors. For example, you will find a map that allows you to study Hannibal's operations in the Punic Wars, and a map of ancient Gaul that will let you follow Caesar's campaigns in his *Commentāriī dē bellō Gallicō*. Two maps show the mythical voyages of Odysseus and Aeneas.

In each chapter of the book you will find a map accompanied by a short essay. The essay is followed by exercises intended to help you master the important features of the map. The answers to most of the exercises can be found in the essay or on the map itself. Some of the exercises ask questions in Latin, and a translation of those questions can be found at the end of each chapter.

One exercise in every section asks you to go beyond the information contained in the book. This exercise is always labeled *Īre ulterius*. The phrase *Īre ulterius* means "going or to go further," and you will need a dictionary, an encyclopedia, a history book, or the Internet to find the answers to these questions. In addition to the exercises, each chapter provides suggestions for projects.

Before turning to the maps of the Roman *orbis terrārum* (world), you should know the Latin words for north, south, east, and west. The Latin word for north is *septentriōnēs* because Septentriōnēs was the Latin name of the constellation we call the Big Dipper, and the North Star can be located by following an imaginary line from the far edge of the bowl of the dipper. Boreās and Aquīlo are winds that blow from the north so their names are sometimes used to mean north. The Latin word *merīdiēs*, which often means noon or midday, is also used to mean south since the sun is visible to the south at noon. *Oriens*, the Latin word for east, comes from the verb *orior* (to rise) because, of course, the sun rises in the east. Similarly, *solis occāsus* means west as well as sunset, since the sun sets in the west. *Occidēns* (setting) is another way of saying west, as is Zephyrus, the name of the west wind.

EXERCISES

I. Label the compass rose below using the Latin words *septentriōnēs, merīdiēs, oriens, occidēns*:

II. Match the Latin words with their English meanings. You will need to use some of the English words more than once.

1. _____ Boreās   A. map

2. _____ Zephyrus   B. world

3. _____ oriens   C. north

4. _____ occidēns   D. south

5. _____ septentriōnēs   E. east

6. _____ merīdiēs   F. west

7. _____ solis occāsus

8. _____ orbis terrārum

9. _____ charta

10. _____ Aquīlo

III. Īre ulterius (going further)

1. What are the two Greek words from which the English word geography comes? Find three English derivatives from each Greek word.

_____

_____

_____

2. In Latin, the word *charta* means map. What is a cartographer? Hint: omit the letter "h" in *charta*.

_____

_____

3. *Charta* sometimes simply means a piece of paper. What does the phrase *magna charta* mean in Latin? What does Magna Carta mean to English historians?

_____

_____

_____

4. What does the Latin phrase *orbis terrārum* mean literally? What did the lands known to the Romans encircle? What does the English word orb mean?

_____

_____

_____

5. Before the American Civil War, slaves in the South sang a song with the words "follow the drinking gourd." What constellation is the "drinking gourd"? What is the Latin word for this constellation? Why would an escaping slave seek to follow this particular constellation?

_____

_____

_____

6. How does the Latin word *septentriōnēs* tell you how many stars make up the Big Dipper? The Big Dipper is part of the constellation *Ursa Māior*. Retell the myth that explains how the *Ursa Māior* came to be in the sky.

   _____

   _____

   _____

7. Boreās is the north wind. What is the English term for the Northern Lights? What is another name for Aurora? Of what was Aurora the goddess?

   _____

   _____

   _____

8. Complete this analogy: orient : east :: occident : _____ .

9. Today we call a book of maps an atlas. Who was Atlas according to ancient mythology? Who were his daughters? Retell the story of the labor of Hercules in which Hercules played a trick on Atlas.

   _____

   _____

   _____

10. The Romans sometimes used the name of a wind to stand for the direction from which the wind blew. Boreās, for example, can mean the north wind or north. What did the Romans call the south wind? What continent takes its name from the south wind?

   _____

   _____

   _____

I. Italia Antīqua
Ancient Italy

Volcanoes, mountains, rivers, oh my! The peninsula of Italy has them all. Look at the map. First, notice the Latin words for some familiar geographical terms: *mōns* means mountain (*montēs* is the plural), and *mare* means sea. Now, notice two living volcanoes, Vesuvius Mōns, whose eruption destroyed Pompēiī in 79 CE, and Aetna Mōns on the island of Sicilia (Sicily). Finally, see how the Alpēs Montēs (the Alps) form a natural barrier in northern Italy, and the Āppennīnus Mōns (the Apennines) run like a spine down the center of the Italian peninsula. Incidentally, the English word peninsula comes from the Latin *paene* meaning almost, and *insula* meaning island.

The island of Sicilia was sometimes called Trīnacria because of its triangular shape. Sicily is separated from the Italian peninsula by the rapidly flowing Fretum Siculum (Strait of Messina). If you have studied mythology, you know that the mythological monsters Scylla and Charybdis were supposed to lurk here, endangering any mariner bold enough to enter the treacherous waters of the strait. These physical barriers of mountains and seas explain why many towns and districts in Italy remained separate entities from ancient times until the unification of Italy in the late nineteenth century.

Have you noticed that each part of the Mediterranean Sea has its own name? The Mare Tyrrhēnum (the Tyrrhenian Sea) is the portion of the Mediterranean that lies to the west of the Italian mainland. Two islands mark the boundary of the Mare Tyrrhēnum. Corsica, the northern island, today belongs to France while Sardinia, the southern island, belongs to Italy.

Other specially named areas of the Mediterranean include the Mare Īonium (the Ionian Sea), which lies southeast of Sicily, and the Mare Ādriāticum (the Adriatic Sea), which is located between Italy and Greece. Ādriāticum is sometimes spelled beginning with an "H" in Latin. It thus becomes Hadriatic in English.

It is interesting to note that Rōma (Rome) lies about fifteen miles inland from the Mare Tyrrhēnum. The town of Ostia at the mouth of the Tiberis (Tiber River) served as the port of Rome. Another busy port on the west coast of Italy was Neāpolis, the city we call Naples. You can find Neāpolis about one hundred forty miles south of Rome. On the Adriatic coast, Brundisium (Brindisi) was the point of departure for goods and travelers going to Greece.

Rivers were vital arteries of travel and commerce in the ancient world. You can see that the Tiber connected Rome with her port city Ostia. Rivers also marked boundaries. In northeastern Italy, for example, the river Padus divided northern Italy from the territory called Gallia Transalpīna (Gaul Across the Alps, i.e., modern France). Today, we call this river the Po.

A smaller river in northeastern Italy, the Rubicō (Rubicon), was another important dividing line. A Roman general was not permitted to bring his army south of the Rubicon into central Italy without permission of the Senate. You may have heard the expression "to cross the Rubicon." It means to make an irrevocable decision, and it comes from an actual event in Roman history. When Iūlius Caesar crossed the Rubicon in 49 BCE, he knew that his action would lead to a civil war, and there would be no turning back. As he made the fateful decision to cross the Rubicon, he is supposed to have said "Ālea iacta est!" ("The die has been cast!") *Ālea* means one of a pair of dice so Caesar's words seem to show that he saw crossing the Rubicon as a gamble.

In addition to the physical features of Italy, it is interesting to note the location of several regions that were important in ancient times. Etrūria is the area northwest of Rome once controlled by a highly civilized people called the Etruscans. Rome itself is in the region known as Latium (Lazio) while the area around Pompēiī was called Campānia. Āpūlia (Puglia) refers to the largely agricultural region on the south coast of the Adriatic, birthplace of the poet Horace. All of southern Italy plus the island of Sicily was originally colonized by people from Greece so it was called Magna Graecia, "Great(er) Greece."

Note that this map shows the boundaries of the administrative districts established during the Augustan period.

EXERCISES

I. Highlight the following on the map:

1. Rōma (Rome)
2. Ostia
3. Neāpolis (Naples)
4. Pompēiī
5. Brundisium (Brindisi)
6. Āppennīnus Mōns (Appenines)
7. Alpēs Montēs (Alps)
8. Vesuvius Mōns (Mt. Vesuvius)
9. Aetna Mōns (Mt. Etna)
10. Corsica
11. Sardinia
12. Sicilia (Sicily)
13. Mare Tyrrhēnum (Tyrrhenian Sea)
14. Mare Īonium (Ionian Sea)
15. Mare (H)Ādriāticum (Adriatic Sea)
16. Fretum Siculum (Strait of Messina)
17. Tiberis (Tiber)
18. Padus (Po)
19. Rubicō (Rubicon)
20. Etrūria
21. Latium (Lazio)
22. Campānia
23. Āpūlia (Puglia)
24. Magna Graecia (Southern Italy and Sicily)

Ancient Italy

Septentriōnēs
Occidēns — Oriens
Meridiēs

ALPĒS MONTĒS

Padus

Illyricum

Ā P P E N N Ī N U S

Rubicō

Etrūria

Tiberis

Corsica

Rōma

Ostia

Latium

Mare (H)Ādriāticum

M
Ō
N
S

Āpūlia

Brundisium

Vesuvius Mōns
Neāpolis ● ▲
● Pompēiī

Campānia

Sardinia

Mare
Tyrrhēnum

Magna
Graecia

Mare
Īonium

Aetna Mōns ▲
Fretum
Siculum

Sicilia

Carthāgō ●

Africa

0   100 miles
0   100 km

© 2010 Bolchazy-Carducci Publishers, Inc.

II.   Respondē breviter Latīnē.

1.   Quis dīxit "Ālea iacta est"?

_____

2.   Quid haec verba Anglicē (in English) significant: *mōns, mare, paene*?

_____

3.   Ubi Scylla et Charybdis habitābant?

_____

4.   Ubi est Latium?

_____

5.   Ubi est Etrūria?

_____

6.   Quid est nōmen alterum īnsulae Siciliae?

_____

III.   Match:

1.   _____   port of Rome   A.   Alpēs

2.   _____   river of Rome   B.   Latium

3.   _____   large port near Mt. Vesuvius   C.   Tiberis

4.   _____   sea between Italy and Greece   D.   Pompēiī

5.   _____   river crossed by Caesar in 49 BCE   E.   Neāpolis

6.   _____   Adriatic port in southeastern Italy   F.   Sicilia

7.   _____   large triangular island   G.   (H)Ādriāticum

8.   _____   volcano in Sicily   H.   Campānia

9.   _____   lofty northern mountain range   I.   Aetna Mōns

10. _____   city buried by volcanic eruption   J.   Ostia

11. _____   area around Rome   K.   Rubicō

12. _____   area around Pompeii   L.   Brundisium

IV. Review by giving the Latin name for each.

1. Rome _____

2. the river of Rome _____

3. the port of Rome _____

4. the volcano that buried Pompeii _____

5. a living volcano in Sicily _____

6. the river Caesar crossed with his army in 49 BCE _____

7. two islands west of Rome _____

8. the large triangular island south of the Italian peninsula _____

9. the sea to the west of Rome _____

10. the sea between Italy and Greece _____

11. the sea southwest of Sicily _____

12. the mountain range that runs like a spine down the Italian peninsula _____

13. the lofty mountain range in the north of Italy _____

14. the strait separating Sicily from the mainland _____

V. Tell where each of the following is located in relation to the city of Rome.

e.g., Alps   north

1. Neāpolis   _____

2. Corsica   _____

3. Pompēiī   _____

4. Brundisium   _____

5. Rubicō   _____

6. Sicilia   _____

7. Mare Tyrrhēnum   _____

VI.   Test yourself! Label the blank map with the following:

1. Rōma (Rome)
2. Ostia
3. Neāpolis (Naples)
4. Pompēiī (Pompeii)
5. Brundisium (Brindisi)
6. Āppennīnus Mōns (Apennines)
7. Alpēs Montēs (Alps)
8. Vesuvius Mōns (Mt. Vesuvius)
9. Aetna Mōns (Mt. Etna)
10. Corsica
11. Sardinia

12. Sicilia (Sicily)
13. Mare Tyrrhēnum (Tyrrhenian Sea)
14. Mare Īonium (Ionian Sea)
15. Mare (H)Ādriāticum (Adriatic Sea)
16. Fretum Siculum (Messina)
17. Tiberis (Tiber)
18. Rubicō (Rubicon)
19. Etrūria (Etruria)
20. Latium (Lazio)
21. Campānia (Campania)
22. Magna Graecia (Southern Italy and Sicily)

VII. Īre ulterius

1. The Via Appia was the earliest of the great Roman roads. Find out when the Via Appia was built, what cities it connected initially, and where its later extension led.

_____

_____

_____

2. What does the Latin word *ōs* mean? What does *ostium* mean? How are those words related to the name of the port of Rome?

_____

_____

3. What mythological beings were supposed to live and work in Mt. Aetna? Why was this an appropriate place for them to work? When is the last time Mt. Aetna erupted?

_____

_____

_____

4. *Ālea* means "die" in English. What is the plural of "die"? How would you translate the name of a Roman racehorse called Āleator?

_____

_____

ANCIENT ITALY

5. The Roman poet Vergil was born in Northern Italy, but he died in Brundisium and was buried in Naples. He died just after his return from a journey on which he had fallen ill. What country had he probably visited on this last journey if he died in Brundisium? What is the modern name for Brundisium?

_____

_____

6. Find information about the monsters Scylla and Charybdis. Describe each. Why is it appropriate that they are associated with the treacherous Strait of Messina? Find the town of Scilla on a modern map of Southern Italy, and explain where it is located.

_____

_____

_____

7. One of Rome's greatest foes was the city of Carthāgō (Carthage). Find Carthāgō on the map and describe its location.

_____

_____

8. Centuries after the fall of Rome the French emperor Napoleon was born on the island of Corsica. He was exiled to the island of Elba. Find Elba on a map, and tell where it is located.

_____

_____

VIII. Ancient Italy Projects

1. Make a relief map of ancient Italy. Use papier-mâché or quick drying clay to create mountains. Label the mountains, rivers, islands, cities, and seas in Latin. Include the Via Appia. Use color! Don't forget to include a compass rose and a legend.

2. Design a short booklet with illustrations of the monsters associated with Aetna and Messina. You should have one depiction of Mt. Etna, one of the Strait of Messina, one of Scylla, one of Charybdis, and one of the Cyclopes. Label each illustration and include one sentence in Latin about what it represents, e.g., *Cyclōpēs Vulcānum iūvābant*. Have your teacher check your sentences before you put them on the illustrations!

3. Make a comic strip of at least five panels showing Caesar's crossing of the Rubicon River. Include an image of Caesar saying, "Ālea iacta est."

4. Copy the image of the three-legged symbol of Trīnacria (Sicily) as a poster or recreate it as a plaque in quick drying clay.

5. Use Google Images to find illustrations of Greek remains in Southern Italy and in Sicily. Paestum, Selinunte, Agrigento, Syracusa, and Taormina all have a variety of interesting archeological sites. Prepare a poster with images of temples, theaters, and other ruins that you have found. Label the images. Include on the poster a map of Italy with Paestum, Selinunte, Agrigento, Syracusa, and Taormina clearly marked.

6. Use Google Images to find illustrations of the mosaics found at Piazza Armerina in Sicily. Prepare a poster with images of 5–10 of the mosaics.

ANCIENT ITALY CERTAMEN

1. What is the port of Rome?

    Bonus 1: What is the river of Rome?

    Bonus 2: Name the area around ancient Rome.

2. Name a living volcano on the island of Sicily.

    Bonus 1: What is the ancient name for Naples?

    Bonus 2: Name a city destroyed by the eruption of Mt. Vesuvius in 79 CE.

3. From what Italian seaport do Romans depart for Greece?

    Bonus 1: What sea will one cross to go from Italy to Greece?

    Bonus 2: Give an alternate spelling for Adriatic.

4. What sea lies between Italy and the islands of Corsica and Sardinia?

    Bonus 1: Which island, Corsica or Sardinia, is closer to modern France?

    Bonus 2: Which island, Corsica or Sardinia, is a region of modern Italy?

5. Sumus monstra. Inter Italiam et Siciliam habitāmus. Quae sumus?

    Bonus 1: Name the strait between Italy and Sicily.

    Bonus 2: Name the sea southeast of Sicily.

6. What was the area around Pompeii called?

    Bonus 1: What do we call the area northwest of Rome?

    Bonus 2: What mysterious people once controlled Etruria?

7. Ubi sunt Alpēs Montēs?

    Bonus 1: What is the nominative singular of the Latin word for mountain?

    Bonus 2: Name the mountain range that runs almost the whole length of the Italian peninsula.

8. Why was the Rubicon River an important boundary to Roman generals?

    Bonus 1: In what year did Caesar cross the Rubicon?

    Bonus 2: What resulted from his crossing the Rubicon with his army?

9. What famous Latin phrase is Caesar supposed to have said when he crossed the Rubicon?

    Bonus 1: Translate the phrase into English.

    Bonus 2: Why might Caesar have considered that crossing the Rubicon was a gamble?

10. What does the Latin word *paene* mean?

    Bonus 1: What is the Latin word for island?

    Bonus 2: What is the Latin word for a body of land surrounded on three sides by water?

11. What do we call the constellation the Romans called Septentriōnēs?

    Bonus 1: What is another meaning for septentriōnēs?

    Bonus 2: Why is the constellation associated with north?

12. Give the Latin name of a wind that blows from the north.

    Bonus 1: Name another wind that blows from the north.

    Bonus 2: Name the wind whose name sometimes means west.

13. Translate the Latin word *occidēns*.

    Bonus 1 & 2: Give two English meanings for the Latin phrase *sōlis occāsus*.

14. Give the Latin word that means south.

    Bonus 1: What is another meaning of *merīdiēs*?

    Bonus 2: Give the Latin word that means east.

15. What is the Latin phrase that means world?

    Bonus 1: What part of Italy was known as Magna Graecia?

    Bonus 2: What is the Latin word for "sea"?

TRANSLATION OF EXERCISE II

Respondē breviter Latīnē = Answer briefly in Latin.

1. Quis dīxit "Ālea iacta est"? = Who said "The die is cast?"

2. Quid haec verba Anglicē (in English) significant: *mōns, mare, paene*? = What do these words mean in English?

3. Ubi Scylla et Charybdis habitābant? = Where did Scylla and Charybdis used to live?

4. Ubi est Latium? = Where is Latium?

5. Ubi est Etrūria? = Where is Etruria?

6. Quid est nōmen alterum īnsulae Siciliae? = What is another name for the island of Sicily?

II. Orbis Terrārum Rōmānus
The Roman World

It is easy to see why "Mediterranean" is an appropriate name for the sea that lies in the middle (*medius*) of the land (*terra*) that was once controlled by Rome. The Romans themselves called the Mediterranean Mare Nostrum (our sea) because their dominions did indeed encircle it. Of course, at its greatest extent, during the reign of the Emperor Trajan in the second century, the Roman Empire actually stretched well beyond the Mediterranean basin.

Let's begin our tour of the Roman world by revisiting Italia. Be sure that you can locate Rōma, Ostia, Pompēiī, and Brundisium. Can you also find the Tiberis and the Rubicō rivers and the Alpēs Montēs? Look for the islands of Corsica, Sardinia, and Sicilia. Remember that the Mare Tyrrhēnum lies between the Italian peninsula and the islands of Corsica and Sardinia while the Mare (H)Ādriāticum separates Italia from Graecia (Greece), and the Mare Īonium is east of Sicilia.

Now, let's look more closely at Graecia. The northern part of the Greek peninsula, called Macedonia, was home to Alexander the Great. North and east of Macedonia you can see Dācia and Thrācia. Today, these are roughly the modern countries of Romania and Bulgaria. To the west the rugged land along the Adriatic coast was an area known to the Romans as Illyricum.

Notice that Athēnae (Athens) is plural in both Latin and English. Notice also that the arm of the Mediterranean east of Athēnae is called the Mare Aegaeum (Aegean Sea). You will find Sparta, the ancient rival of Athēnae, in the southern portion of the Greek peninsula known as the Peloponnēsus. The city of Corinthus (Corinth) is located on the isthmus between the Peloponnēsus and the northern part of the Greek peninsula. An isthmus is a narrow bridge of land that lies between two bodies of water and connects two larger land masses. Today, a canal allows access from the Adriatic to the Aegean, but in ancient times, ships were put on rollers and dragged across the isthmus.

As we continue our tour of the Roman world at the eastern end of the Mediterranean, you will see that the Latin word Asia did not mean the whole continent as it does in English. To a Roman, Asia meant the land mass we call Asia Minor. Note the areas of Asia called Bīthȳnia and Pontus, which lie to the south of the Pontus Euxīnus (Black Sea). Iūlius Caesar won a famous battle in Pontus at Zela in 47 BCE. It was after this victory that he reported "Vēnī, vīdī, vīcī." (I came, I saw, I conquered.)

Bȳzantium, which lies at the southwestern end of the Pontus Euxīnus, was the largest and wealthiest city in Bīthȳnia. Ships bearing goods from the Black Sea and points further east necessarily passed through Bȳzantīum on their way into the Mediterranean. Overland trade routes also passed through the city and led to its growth and strategic importance. Bȳzantium was renamed Constantīnopolis (Constantinople) in the fourth century CE when Constantine made it his capital. Today it is called Istanbul. Interestingly, the name Istanbul is a corruption of the Greek phrase εἰς τὴν πόλιν meaning "to the city." Other famous cities in Asia include Ephesus and Trōia (Troy) also called Īlium. Both lie on the coast of the Aegean Sea. Ephesus was the center of the worship of the goddess Diana whose temple was considered one of the seven wonders of the ancient world, and Trōia is, of course, the site of the Trojan War, famous in the epics of Homer and Vergil.

Southeast of Roman Asia, you can see a large area labeled Syria. The chief city of Syria was Antiochīa (Antioch). Excavations in Antioch have revealed a prosperous city especially notable for its elegant and elaborate mosaics. To the east of Syria lay Parthia, a land whose army was famous for its archers. Here, Caesar's colleague Crassus was defeated at the battle of Carrhae in the year 53 BCE. His defeat was especially disgraceful since the Parthians managed to capture his eagles, the standards of the Roman legions. Augustus recovered the eagles through diplomacy. Today, this area is part of the modern country of Iran. South of Syria, Hierosolyma (Jerusalem) and the port of Caesārea Maritima were important cities in the area known to the Romans as Iūdaea. East of Iūdaea in the region of Arabia, the city of Petra was a vital link for overland trade with the East.

Before we finish our overview of the eastern Mediterranean, it is important to take note of the islands lining the shores of the Aegean. Rhodus (Rhodes) is a large island off the coast of Asia. A famous teacher of rhetoric, Apollōnius Molo, lived on the island of Rhodus, and Iūlius Caesar was kidnapped by pirates on his way to study with him. You may also have heard of the enormous statue that marked the entrance to the harbor of Rhodes. Known as the Colossus of Rhodes, it was considered one of the seven wonders of the ancient world.

It is also important to locate two other large islands, Cyprus and Crēta (Crete). Cyprus was renowned as a center for the worship of the goddess Venus while Crete was famous for the myths of Theseus and the Minotaur. Cnōsos is the site of the legendary labyrinth in which the Minotaur was imprisoned.

Look now at Roman Africa. Just as Asia comprised only part of what we mean today by Asia, so the term Africa referred only to the coastal areas of the continent that border the Mediterranean. The eastern province of Aegyptus (Egypt) was a vital source of grain for the city of Rome. You can find the port city of Alexandrēa, so named to honor Alexander the Great, at the mouth of the Nīlus (Nile). The lighthouse of Alexandrēa was considered one of the seven wonders of the ancient world, and the library of Alexandrēa was famous for generations of scholars. Sadly, the library was destroyed by fire in the first century BCE.

The Rubrum Mare (Red Sea) provided a natural boundary to the east of Aegyptus. To the west, a desert separated Aegyptus from the area the Romans called Libȳa. Cȳrēnē was a major port city in Libȳa. Notice that there are two dangerous sandbanks along this coast: Syrtis Maior and Syrtis Minor. Numidia and Maurītānia are to the west of Libȳa. On the coast of Numidia lies Carthāgō (Carthage), Rome's great enemy in the Punic Wars. When you see how close Carthāgō is to Sicilia, you can understand why the first Punic War involved rival claims to the island by both Rome and Carthage. You can find a detailed map of the most famous campaigns of the Punic Wars later in this book.

After the Punic Wars, Africa became increasingly important to the economy of Rome. The rich harvests of Numidia and Maurītānia filled an ever growing demand for grain. Africa also supplied enormous numbers of exotic animals for the *munera* (gladiatorial games). Crowds throughout the Roman Empire loved spectacles, and large numbers of all sorts of animals were regularly exported through African ports like Carthage to satisfy this popular obsession. Extensive ruins in cities like Volūbilis attest to the prosperity of North Africa under Roman rule. Locate Hippō Rēgius, the birthplace of the historian Suetonius, and Leptis Magna where the late Roman emperor Septimius Severus was born.

The Atlās Mōns (Atlas Mountains) west of Carthage take their name from the mythological Titan Atlās who was said to hold the world on his shoulders. According to the myth, Hercules passed through this part of north Africa on his way to collect the cattle of Geryon. This was the tenth of his twelve labors. He placed the rock of Gibraltar at the entrance to the Mediterranean to help him find his way back to Greece. This story explains why the Rock of Gibraltar was known to the Romans as the Pillars of Hercules.

Just across the Strait of Gibraltar from North Africa lies the Iberian peninsula, which had once been a possession of Carthage. It was added to Rome's dominions after her victory in the Second Punic War. Notice that Hispānia refers to modern Spain, and Lūsitānia to modern Portugal. Ibēria includes both Hispānia and Lūsitānia. You can easily locate Olisīpō (Lisbon) in Lūsitānia and Corduba (Cordova) in Hispānia. The Pȳrēnaeī Montēs (Pyrénées) create a formidable natural boundary between Hispānia and Gallia (France). Note that the Sēquana (Seine) marks the northern limit of Celtic Gaul. The Sēquana (Seine) is the river of Lutetia (Paris) while the port city of Massilia (Marseilles) lies at the mouth of the Rodanus (Rhône).

Britannia (Britain) was invaded twice by Iūlius Caesar, but it did not actually become part of the Roman Empire until the reign of the Emperor Claudius. Calēdonia (Scotland) never became a Roman province, and the Emperor Hadrian built a massive wall of stone to serve as a boundary between Britannia and Calēdonia. The Vallum Hadriānum (Hadrian's Wall) was over seventy miles in length. Hadrian's successor, Antoninus Pius, pushed the frontier farther north and his Vallum Antōnīnum (Antonine Wall), constructed mostly of earth and turf, served briefly as the farthest outpost of Rome in the British Isles. Neither Wallia (Wales) nor Hibernia (Ireland) ever became Roman provinces. Tradition holds that Patrick was a Roman captured and taken as a slave to Hibernia where he converted the Irish to Christianity and sowed seeds for Latin and Latin literature to flourish.

If you now turn back to the continent of Europe, you will notice that the area we call Switzerland was known to the Romans as Helvētia. Similarly the region that now makes up the low countries of Luxembourg, Belgium, and the Netherlands was inhabited by a people called the Belgae. East of the Belgae, you can see the Rhēnus (Rhine), then as now, a major waterway. North of the Rhine lay Germānia. You may know that Caesar was very proud of having built a bridge across the Rhine in order to carry on a campaign in Germany. His bridge impressed the Germānī with the technological prowess of the Romans. Another major river was the Dānuvius (Danube). It flows eastward into the Pontus Euxīnus. Northeast of the Dānuvius bordering the Pontus Euxīnus is Scythia, a land considered remote and barbarous by Roman writers like Catullus.

EXERCISES

I.   Review the following by underlining them on the map:

1. Alpēs Montēs (Alps)
2. Rōma (Rome)
3. Brundisium (Brindisi)
4. Tiberis (Tiber)
5. Italia (Italy)
6. Corsica
7. Sardinia
8. Sicilia (Sicily)
9. Mare Tyrrhēnum (Tyrrhenian Sea)
10. Mare Īonium (Ionian Sea)
11. Mare (H)Ādriāticum (Adriatic Sea)

THE ROMAN WORLD

II.   Now highlight these areas on the map:

1.   Graecia (Greece)

2.   Asia (Asia Minor)

3.   Arabia

4.   Parthia

5.   Iūdaea (Judea)

6.   Africa (North Africa)

7.   Aegyptus(Egypt)

8.   Ibēria (Spain and Portugal)

9.   Hispānia (Spain)

10. Lūsitānia (Portugal)

11. Gallia (France)

12. Britannia (Britain)

13. Calēdonia (Scotland)

14. Hibernia (Ireland)

15. Belgae (Belgium and the Netherlands)

III. Circle these cities:

1.   Bȳzantium (Constantinople/Istanbul)

2.   Hierosolyma (Jerusalem)

3.   Alexandrēa (Alexandria)

4.   Carthāgō (Carthage)

5.   Athēnae (Athens)

6.   Sparta

7.   Trōia (Troy)

IV.   Highlight these mountains, rivers, islands, and bodies of water:

1.   Pȳrēnaeī Montēs (Pyrénées)

2.   Atlās Mōns (Atlas Mountains)

3.   Sēquana (Seine)

4.   Nīlus (Nile)

5.   Crēta (Crete)

6.   Rhodus (Rhodes)

7.   Cyprus

8.   Pontus Euxīnus (Black Sea)

9.   Rubrum Mare (Red Sea)

10. Mare Aegaeum (Aegean Sea)

V.   Respondē breviter Latīnē.

1.   Quis dīxit "Vēnī, vīdī, vīcī"?

_____

2.   Ubi est Mare Aegaeum?

_____

3.   Quis magnum mūrum inter Britanniam et Calēdoniam aedificāvit?

_____

VI. Match the Latin name with the modern name:

1. _____ Calēdonia   A. Romania

2. _____ Hispānia   B. Mediterranean Sea

3. _____ Hibernia   C. France

4. _____ Thrācia   D. Turkey

5. _____ Ibēria   E. Spain

6. _____ Lūsitānia   F. Spain + Portugal

7. _____ Asia   G. Scotland

8. _____ Mare Nostrum   H. Ireland

9. _____ Gallia   I. Portugal

10. _____ Dācia   J. Bulgaria

VII. Tell where each of the following is in relation to the city of Rome.

e.g., Alps   north

1. Gallia   _____

2. Graecia   _____

3. Crēta   _____

4. Athēnae   _____

5. Rhodus   _____

VIII. Explain briefly where each sea is located within the Mediterranean.

1. Tyrrhenian _____

2. (H)Adriatic _____

3. Aegaean _____

4. Ionian _____

IX. Give the English for each sea.

1. Mare Nostrum   _____

2. Rubrum Mare   _____

3. Pontus Euxīnus   _____

THE ROMAN WORLD

X.   Test yourself! Label the blank map with the following:

1. Alpēs Montēs (Alps)
2. Rōma (Rome)
3. Neāpolis (Naples)
4. Brundisium (Brindisi)
5. Tiberis (Tiber)
6. Italia (Italy)
7. Corsica
8. Sardinia
9. Sicilia (Sicily)
10. Mare Tyrrhēnum (Tyrrhenian Sea)
11. Mare Īonium (Ionian Sea)
12. Mare (H)Ādriāticum (Adriatic Sea)
13. Mare Aegaeum (Aegean Sea)
14. Pontus Euxīnus (Black Sea)
15. Mare Rubrum (Red Sea)
16. Asia (Asia Minor)
17. Iūdaea (Judea)
18. Arabia
19. Parthia (Iran)
20. Africa (North Africa)
21. Aegyptus (Egypt)
22. Ibēria (Spain + Portugal)
23. Hispānia (Spain)
24. Gallia (France)
25. Britannia (Britain)
26. Calēdonia (Scotland)
27. Belgae (Belgium + Netherlands)
28. Graecia (Greece)
29. Athēnae (Athens)
30. Sparta
31. Bȳzantium (Istanbul/Constantinople)
32. Hierosolyma (Jerusalem)
33. Alexandrēa (Alexandria)
34. Trōia
35. Crēta
36. Rhodus (Rhodes)
37. Atlās Mōns (Atlas Mountains)
38. Pȳrēnaeī Montēs (Pyrénées Mountains)
39. Sēquana (Seine)
40. Dānuvius (Danube)
41. Nīlus
42. Rhēnus (Rhine)

XI. Īre ulterius

1. Research the derivation of the name of the continent of Europe. Retell the myth briefly.

_____

_____

_____

2. Research the myth of Theseus and the Minotaur. Retell the myth briefly.

_____

_____

_____

3. Find out how the myth of Daedalus is connected to the myth of Theseus. Retell the myth of Daedalus briefly. Be sure to include the name of the island named after Daedalus's son.

_____

_____

_____

4. What does the phrase "parthian shot" mean in English? What is its derivation?

_____

_____

_____

5. What does _euxīnus_ mean? Why was this name given to the Pontus Euxīnus (Black Sea)? What was the area south of the Black Sea called?

_____

_____

_____

6. Whom did the Romans call "Poenī"? For what were the Poenī famous? Where did the Poenī come from originally? What modern country occupies this area today? Name two of the best known cities of the Poenī.

_____

_____

_____

7. Where were the Isthmian Games held? Where were other important athletic games held in ancient Greece? What prizes were awarded at each of the games?

_____

_____

_____

8. Find the definition of the word _vēnātio_ in a Latin dictionary. Make a list of some of the exotic animals imported from Africa for the _mūnera_ in Rome.

_____

_____

_____

XII. Roman World Projects

1. Labors of Hercules Map

Make a list of the Twelve Labors of Hercules. Find the locations of as many of the labors as possible. Then prepare a poster with an enlarged map of the Mediterranean basin. Indicate the location of each of Hercules's labors. Include side adventures like Hercules's encounter with Cacus.

2. List Project

Make a list of as many names as possible of towns or cities in the United States that take their names from the ancient world, e.g., Athens, Georgia, or Troy, New York. You may want to include cities like Indianapolis, not because it is named after an ancient city, but because its name ends with the Greek word polis, meaning city.

3. Postcard Project

Use a small piece of poster board to create the front and back of a postcard from an ancient city, province, or island of the Roman Empire. Write a message on the postcard, and mail it to your teacher.

Front/picture side:

- A map or image of your city or area. Draw it yourself, or use a computer image.
- Latin name of your city or area + modern English name

Back/address side:

- Salutation (e.g., *Salvē Magistra*)
- A note of at least three sentences telling where you are, what direction your location is from Rome, and two facts about your location.
- Your signature
- The address: your teacher's name and your school's address

NB: Instead of making and mailing an actual postcard, this project can be done as a poster. Cut a piece of poster board in half. Use one side for the map or image, the other for the message and address. Design a suitable stamp. Share the other half with a friend. Display the posters in your classroom.

ROMAN WORLD CERTAMEN

1. What sea lies between Italy and Greece?

   Bonus 1: What sea lies east of Sicily?

   Bonus 2: What sea lies between Greece and Asia Minor.

2. What region east of Syria was known in ancient times for its skilled archers?

   Bonus 1: What Roman general was defeated at the battle of Carrhae in Parthia?

   Bonus 2: Who recovered the eagles by using diplomacy?

3.   What is the modern name for Calēdonia?

     Bonus 1: What is the modern name for Lūsitānia?

     Bonus 2: What is the modern name for Gallia?

4.   What did the Romans call Ireland?

     Bonus 1: What did the Romans call Spain?

     Bonus 2: What did the Romans call Spain + Portugal?

5.   Where is Istanbul located?

     Bonus 1 and 2: Give two other names for the city we call Istanbul.

6.   On what island did Apollōnius Molo, the famous teacher of rhetoric, live?

     Bonus 1: What wonder of the ancient world marked the entrance to the harbor of Rhodes?

     Bonus 2: What happened to Iūlius Caesar on his way to the island of Rhodes to study with Apollōnius Molo?

7.   What island is famous for its association with the myth of Theseus?

     Bonus 1: Where was the labyrinth located according to legend?

     Bonus 2: What hero slew the Minotaur?

8.   What is another name for the city of Ilium?

     Bonus 1: What is the modern name for Hierosolyma?

     Bonus 2: What Egyptian city is famous for its lighthouse and its library?

9.   Let's think about rivers of the ancient world. Where was the Nīlus?

     Bonus 1: What is the modern name for the Rhēnus?

     Bonus 2: What is the modern name for the Sēquana?

10. What Roman general invaded Britannia twice, in 55 BCE and again in 54 BCE?

     Bonus 1: What Roman emperor built a stone wall seventy miles long in northern England?

     Bonus 2: What later emperor built another wall farther north than Hadrian's Wall?

11. According to myth, the hero Hercules needed a landmark to help him find his way back to Greece after collecting the cattle of Geryon. How did he mark the entrance to the Mediterranean Sea?

    Bonus 1: What is the modern name for the Pillars of Hercules?

    Bonus 2: What did the Romans call the Mediterranean Sea?

12. Where are the Atlas Mountains?

    Bonus 1: Where are the Alps?

    Bonus 2: Where are the Pyrénées Mountains?

13. Name a Greek city whose name is plural in both English and in Latin.

    Bonus 1: What Greek city lies on the narrow isthmus between the mainland of Greece and the Peloponnese?

    Bonus 2: How did ships in ancient times cross this isthmus?

14. Where is Macedonia?

    Bonus 1: Where is Scythia?

    Bonus 2: Where is Illyricum?

15. What city controlled Spain before it became a Roman province?

    Bonus 1: Where is the city of Carthage?

    Bonus 2: What are the wars between Rome and Carthage called?

TRANSLATION OF EXERCISE V

Respondē breviter Latīnē = Answer briefly in Latin.

1. Quis dīxit "Vēnī, vīdī, vīcī"? = Who said, "I came, I saw, I conquered"?

2. Ubi est Mare Aegaeum? = Where is the Aegean Sea?

3. Quis magnum mūrum inter Britanniam et Calēdoniam aedificāvit? = Who built a big wall between England and Scotland?

III. Viae Rōmānae
Roman Roads

When you consider the extent of Rome's dominions, you may well wonder how officials in Rome were able to control such a vast empire. The answer is, of course, that an elaborate network of roads connected Rome to her far-flung territories.

You will find the earliest of the great Roman roads in central Italy. Called by the Romans the "Rēgīna Viārum" (the Queen of Roads), the Via Appia, was begun in 312 BCE by Appius Claudius Caecus, a Roman magistrate who recognized the importance of creating a link between Rome and her newly acquired possessions in southern Italy. Initially the Via Appia connected Rome with the town of Capua, but it was later extended over the Āppennīnus Mōns to the port of Brundisium. Some parts of it are still in use today, more than two thousand years later!

In addition to the Via Appia, another ancient road, the Via Latīna, provided access to southern Italy. To the north, the Via Flāminia connected Rome with the Adriatic coast, as did the Via Salāria. The Via Aemilia led to the area near Mediolānum (Milan) while the Via Aurēlia linked Rome with Genua (Genoa).

As Rome's empire grew, additional roads were built both in Italy and in the provinces. Eventually nearly 100,000 miles of paved roads stretched from northern England to Mesopotamia. A well-maintained road system was essential for swift and efficient troop movement, and most of the building of Roman roads fell to the military. When a new road was planned, army engineers laid out the route using a surveying instrument called a *grōma* to ensure a straight course. They planned bridges over valleys and tunnels through hills in order to keep the road as straight as possible. After the route had been determined, soldiers went to work digging a foundation five to ten feet deep and fifteen to twenty feet wide. Large stones in the bottom layer (*pavīmentum*) were covered first with large stones (*statūmen*), next with smaller stones and rubble (*rūdus*), and then with a layer of sand (*nucleus*). Finally paving stones called the *summa crusta* or *summum dorsum* were laid to form the road surface. A cart called a hodometer provided an exact measure of mileage so that mile posts could be set up. These mile posts marked the distance from the *milliārium aureum* (golden milestone), a monument near the Cūria (Senate House) in the Forum at Rome.

ROMAN ROADS OF ITALY

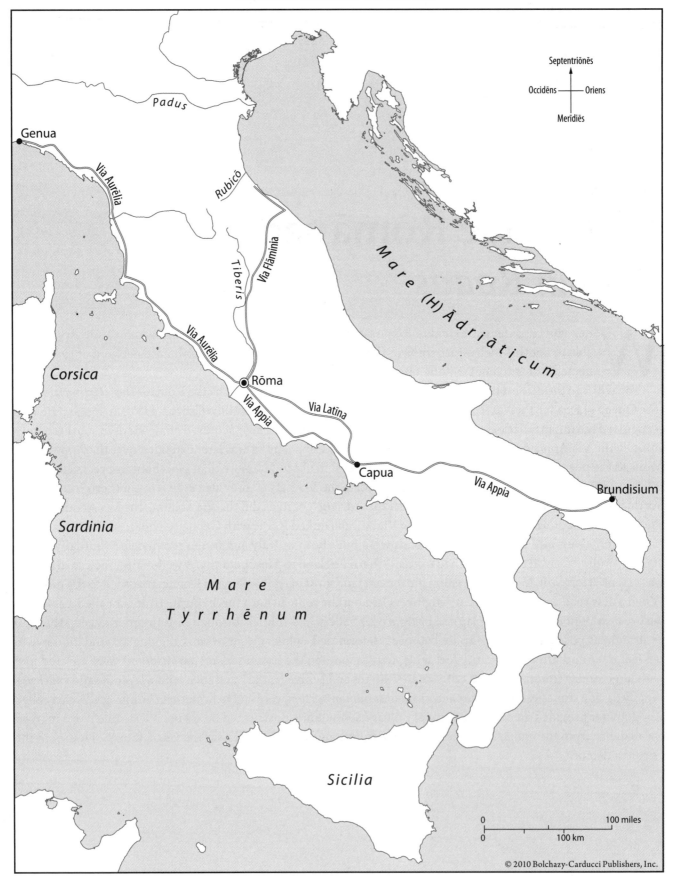

Exercises

I. Highlight on the map of Italy:

1. Via Appia
2. Via Flāminia
3. Via Aurēlia
4. Via Aemilia
5. Rōma
6. Ostia
7. Tusculum
8. Capua
9. Brundisium
10. Tiberis
11. Rubicō
12. Corsica
13. Sardinia
14. Sicilia

II. Highlight on the map of the Roman Empire:

1. Rōma
2. Hispānia
3. Gallia
4. Africa
5. Aegyptus
6. Asia
7. Bȳzantīum
8. Pontus Euxīnus
9. Macedonia
10. Rhēnus
11. Dānuvius
12. Nīlus
13. Mare (H)Ādriāticum
14. Mare Tyrrhēnum

III. Give the Latin for each of the following.

1. Rome   _____
2. Spain   _____
3. Gaul   _____
4. Egypt   _____
5. Black Sea   _____
6. Adriatic Sea   _____

ROADS OF ROMAN EMPIRE

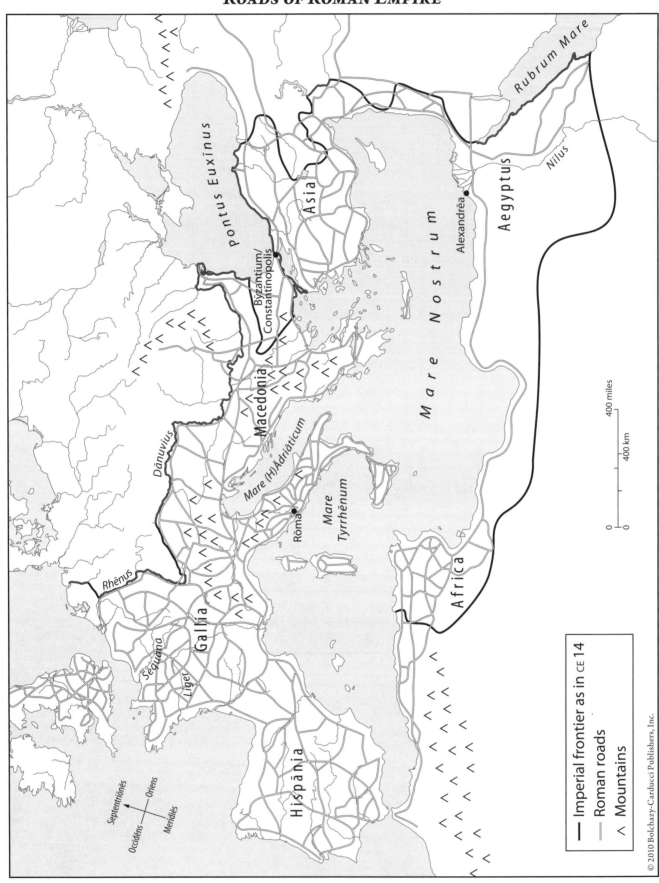

Rubrum Mare

Pontus Euxīnus

Asia

Aegyptus

Nīlus

Alexandrēa

Mare Nostrum

Byzantium/
Constantinopolis

Macedonia

Dānuvius

Mare (H)Ādriāticum

Mare
Tyrrhēnum

Rōma

Africa

Rhēnus

Gallia

Sequana

Liger

Hispānia

Septentriōnēs

Oriens

Occidēns

Merīdiēs

400 miles

400 km

0

0

Imperial frontier as in CE 14

Roman roads

Mountains

© 2010 Bolchazy-Carducci Publishers, Inc.

IV.   Respondē breviter Latīnē.

1.   Ubi erat Milliārium Aureum?

_____

2.   Quid est "Rēgīna Viārum"?

_____

3.   Quot strata (layers) viae Rōmānae habuērunt?

_____

4.   Quī viās Rōmānās aedificābant?

_____

5.   Quid est instrumentum factum ad viās metandās (to measure out)?

_____

V.   Īre ulterius

1.   How long was a Roman mile? How do you say "mile" in Latin?

_____

_____

_____

2.   Find out more about the life of Appius Claudius. Be sure to include the reason he was called *Caecus* and what the office of a censor involved.

_____

_____

_____

3.   What is the origin of the word "Salāria"? What is an English derivative? What does the phrase "*cum granō sālis*" mean? What connection did the Via Salāria have with salt?

_____

_____

_____

4. Find out what a *grōma* looked like. What were the weights on the *grōma* called? What English words come from that Latin word?

    _____

    _____

    _____

5. Use Google Images to find an illustration of a Roman hodometer, and write a brief description. How did it make exact measurements? What is an English word related to "hodometer"?

    _____

    _____

    _____

6. Use Google Images to find pictures of the *milliārum aureum* in Rome and of the Zero Milestone located in Washington, DC. Describe each monument.

    _____

    _____

    _____

7. Translate this Latin phrase into English: *Omnēs viae Rōmam ducunt.*

    _____

VI. Roman Road Projects

1. Road Map of the Roman Empire

    Enlarge the map of the roads of the Roman Empire so that the image fills a full size piece of poster board. Label important cities, regions, islands, and the named portions of the Mediterranean Sea. Use bright colors for the roads. Include a legend and a compass rose. Title your map "*Omnēs viae Rōmam ducunt*" or "All Roads Lead to Rome."

NB: If your classroom has a suitable wall, your teacher might allow you to create your empire map as a large mural. If there are rules about painting directly on the classroom wall, you could consider using a plain white shower curtain that can be hung on the wall.

2. Roman Road in a Box

You will need the following:

- clear plastic box such as those for food storage found in a grocery store
- graham crackers
- marshmallows
- M & Ms™
- Rice Krispies™ cereal
- plain chocolate bar

Arrange the ingredients carefully in five layers. Print a label with the information below and attach it to the side of the box so that the five layers of a Roman road are clearly visible:

- pavīmentum = graham cracker
- statūmen = marshmallows
- rūdus = M & Ms™
- nucleus = Rice Krispies™
- summa crusta, summum dorsum = squares of chocolate bar

Translation of Exercise IV

Respondē breviter Latīnē = Answer briefly in Latin.

1. Ubi erat Milliārium Aureum? = Where was the Golden Milestone?

2. Quid est "Rēgīna Viārum"? = What is the "Queen of Roads"?

3. Quot strata (layers) viae Rōmānae habuērunt? = How many layers did Roman roads have?

4. Quī viās Rōmānās aedificābant? = Who built the Roman roads?

5. Quid est instrumentum factum ad viās metandās (to measure out)? = What is the tool made to measure out roads?

IV. Urbs Rōmae
The City of Rome

Seven Hills and a River

The city of Rome began as a humble village clinging to the slopes of the Mōns Palātīnus (Palatine Hill) near the Tiberis (Tiber River). This early settlement is known as Rōma Quadrāta because its walls encircled the Mōns Palātīnus roughly in the shape of a square. The Forum lies outside this early fortification at the foot of the Mōns Palātīnus where the ground was too swampy for building. In fact, the valley of the Forum served as a burial ground until the sixth century BCE when the Cloāca Maxima, a storm sewer, was constructed to drain the marsh.

As Rome grew, it expanded to encompass other settlements on neighboring hills. According to tradition, the sixth king of Rome, Servius Tullius, enclosed all seven hills with a new set of fortifications, known as the Mūrus Servius (Servian Wall). If you look at the city plan, you can easily locate the seven hills of Servius's city. The Mōns Palātīnus and the outline of Rōma Quadrāta are in the center of the plan. The Mōns Capitōlīnus (Capitoline Hill) lies to the west of the Mōns Palātīnus across the Forum valley. North of the Mōns Capitōlīnus stands the Collis Quirīnālis (the Quirinal Hill) and the Collis Vīminālis (the Viminal Hill). To the east are the Mōns Esquilīnus (the Esquiline Hill) and the Mōns Caelius (the Caelian Hill), while the Mōns Aventīnus (the Aventine Hill) is south of Rōma Quadrāta. It is perhaps worth pointing out that centuries of building and rebuilding combined with natural erosion have eaten away at the famed seven hills until today they appear more as gentle inclines than as significant hills.

Not far from the center of Rōma Quadrāta you can see the Tiberis (Tiber River), which provided a vital link with Ostia, the harbor of Rome. Ostia was at the mouth of the Tiberis on the Mare Tyrrhēnum. Goods from all over the Mediterranean world came into Ostia and were loaded onto barges for the twenty-mile trip up the river to Rome. Warehouses and docks lined the banks of the Tiberis southeast of the Īnsula Tiberīna (Tiber Island). The island was connected to the city of Rome by the Pōns Fabricius, one of the oldest bridges in the city. Another ancient bridge, the Pōns Cēstius, allowed access to the Iāniculum, the hill across the Tiber from the city.

North of the Īnsula Tiberīna you will notice a large open area labeled Campus Martius. Originally, this field outside the Servian Wall served as a parade and exercise area for the Roman army. "Martius" derives from the name of Mars, the Roman god of war, whose altar was built here. The Campus Martius was also the site of citizen assemblies where voting took place. In later times, the Campus Martius ceased to be an open space and was divided into city blocks.

EXERCISES

I.   List the seven hills of Rome.

NB: Some people find this mnemonic helpful. The first letter of each word in this nonsense sentence will give you the first letter of each hill: "Can Queen Victoria eat cold apple pie?"

1.   _____

2.   _____

3.   _____

4.   _____

5.   _____

6.   _____

7.   _____

II. Highlight the seven hills on your city plan; then highlight the Forum, the Tiberis, Īnsula Tiberīna, the Iāniculum, and the Campus Martius.

III. Fill in the blanks.

1.   The earliest use of the valley that became the Forum was _____.

2.   Rōma Quadrāta refers to _____.

3.   The port of Rome is _____, which lies on the _____ Sea.

4.   The Roman army once exercised on the _____.

5.   The Iāniculum is _____.

CITY OF ROME: SEVEN HILLS SCHEMATIC

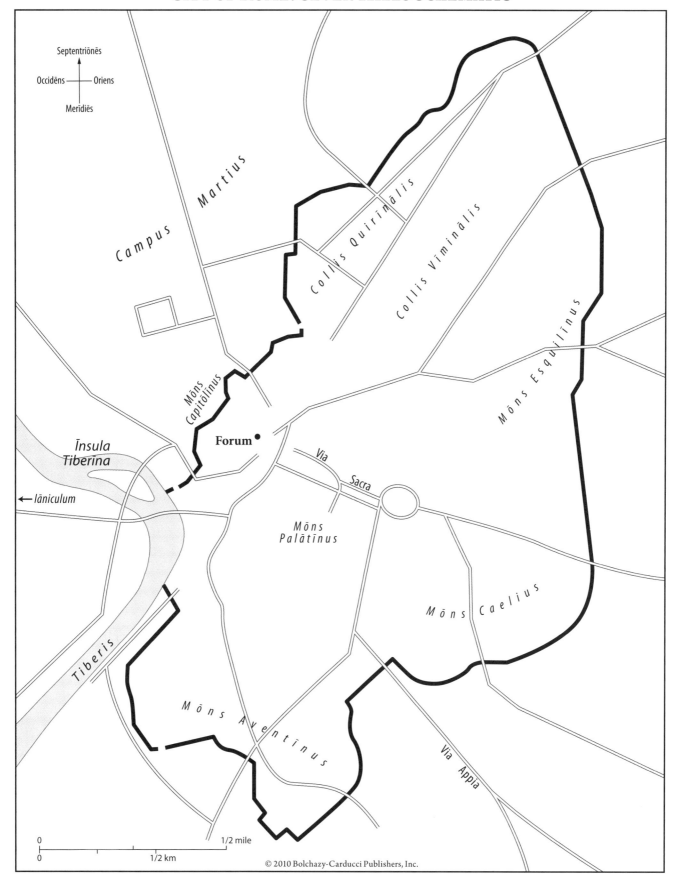

Septentriōnēs

Occidēns ——|—— Oriens

Merīdiēs

Campus Martius

Collis Quirīnālis

Collis Vīminālis

Mōns Esquilīnus

Mōns Capitōlīnus

Forum •

Īnsula Tiberīna

← *Iāniculum*

Via

Sacra

Mōns Palātīnus

Mōns Caelius

Tiberis

Mōns Aventīnus

Via Appia

0   1/2 mile

0   1/2 km

IV. Īre ulterius

1. Find out why Tiber Island has the shape of a ship.

   _____

   _____

2. Describe Iānus, the Roman deity, whose name is related to "Iāniculum." What is the modern Italian name for the area of Rome that includes the Iāniculum? Hint: the name means "across the Tiber."

   _____

   _____

3. Why did the Plebeians leave the city of Rome in 287 BCE and march to the Iāniculum?

   _____

   _____

4. What did a flag raised on the Iāniculum mean during the late Republic? What great Roman orator refers to this tradition in an oration?

   _____

   _____

5. Rome is sometimes called *Urbs Aeterna*. What does *Urbs Aeterna* mean? Another phrase that is used to refer to Rome is *Caput Mundī*. What does *Caput Mundī* mean?

   _____

   _____

V. Test yourself! Label the blank map with the following:

   1. Mōns Caelius (Caelian Hill)
   2. Collis Quirīnālis (Quirinal Hill)
   3. Collis Vīminālis (Viminal Hill)
   4. Mōns Esqulīnus (Esquiline Hill)
   5. Mōns Capitōlīnus (Capitoline Hill)
   6. Mōns Aventīnus (Aventine Hill)
   7. Mōns Palātīnus (Palatine Hill)
   8. Tiberis (Tiber River)
   9. Īnsula Tiberīna (Tiber Island)
   10. Forum
   11. Iāniculum (Janiculum Hill)
   12. Campus Martius

CITY OF ROME: SEVEN HILLS SCHEMATIC

Districts and Landmarks

Let us look now at the districts of the ancient city of Rome. Just south of Ínsula Tiberína were two markets, the Forum Boārium where cattle were sold and the Forum Olitōrium where olive oil, vegetables, and herbs were for sale. Nearby, the Mōns Palātīnus was the site of elegant town houses including that of Livia, the wife of the first emperor Augustus. Eventually, the whole Mōns Palātīnus was almost completely covered by an enormous palace for the emperor's family. In fact, the English word palace is derived from the word Palatine.

The Forum lies in the valley between Mōns Capitōlīnus and the Mōns Palātīnus. You have learned that this marshy area was unsuitable for building until it was drained by a storm sewer called the Cloāca Maxima. You can see a dotted line on the city plan showing where the sewer emptied into the Tiberis just south of the Ínsula Tiberína near the Pōns Aemilius. Interestingly, the Cloāca Maxima still functions today as a storm drain.

East of the Forum, a less prestigious but still prosperous neighborhood grew up on the Mōns Esquilīnus. Here, Cicero's family had a house. At the foot of the Collis Quirīnālis and Collis Vīminālis lay the area known as the Subūra, a crowded and poverty stricken neighborhood of enormous apartment houses called *insulae*. These buildings were notorious for their shoddy construction. Sometimes whole buildings were known to collapse. The Subūra was also vulnerable to fire, and in the nearby Forum of Augustus a substantial wall was built to provide protection against fires originating in the Subūra. The large stone blocks of this fire wall are still visible today.

Many of the inhabitants of the Subūra undoubtedly enjoyed the free gladiatorial shows at the Colossēum just outside of the Forum. This huge amphitheater seating 54,000 people stood on the site of an artificial lake, a decorative element in a park that surrounded Nero's Domus Aurea (Golden House). Nero built the Domus Aurea following the Great Fire of 64 CE. After Nero's death, the pool was drained and much of the Domus Aurea destroyed. The Colossēum was constructed here by the emperor Vespasian, who wanted to provide entertainment for crowds of people instead of pleasure for a single tyrant. The Colossēum is sometimes called the Flavian Amphitheater because Vespasian was a member of the Flavian family. The building's more familiar name of Colossēum comes from its proximity to an enormous statue that once stood near the amphitheater. This huge statue originally depicted Nero, but it was later reworked to represent the sun god. The statue no longer exists, but its colossal size gave the amphitheater its name.

Like the Colossēum, the Stadium of Domitian near the Panthēon provided a venue for gladiatorial spectacles. Today, the contour of the buildings of the Piazza Navona follows the outline of this stadium, and one can view the Roman substructures of the stadium in the lower level of one of the modern buildings at one end of the piazza.

Chariot races were also enormously popular in ancient Rome. Crowds flocked to the Circus Maximus, the great racetrack, which was located in the valley between the Aventine and Palatine Hills. A balcony of the imperial palace on the Palatine was actually constructed so that the imperial family could enjoy the best possible view of the races. In the Campus Martius, the Circus Flāminius was another popular race track, but no trace of it remains today.

Theater productions were another popular diversion in ancient Rome. One of the largest theaters in Rome was built by the Emperor Augustus. Located near the western end of the Circus Maximus, it was named for Augustus's nephew and known as the Theater of Marcellus. After the fall of Rome, the Theater of Marcellus became a palace for the powerful Orsini family. Today, the footprint of the building still retains the shape of the ancient theater.

Gladiatorial games, chariot races, and theater productions provided entertainment on special occasions, but a visit to the *thermae* (public baths) was part of daily life for many of the inhabitants of ancient Rome. The *thermae* were enormous complexes that combined the features of a spa, a country club, and a shopping mall. *Thermae* housed hot and cold swimming pools and saunas, as well as libraries, game rooms, and facilities for playing ball. The baths were free or cost only a token entry fee. Two of the most luxurious *thermae* in Rome, the Baths of Diocletian and the Baths of Caracalla, were built by the emperors whose names they bear.

Augustus's friend and supporter Agrippa was responsible for the construction of another Roman landmark, the Panthēon. Located in the Campus Martius district not far from the Circus Flāminius, this world famous circular temple was dedicated to the twelve Olympian gods. It is especially known for its huge dome, which is 142 feet in diameter. The highest point of the dome is 142 feet from the floor. The present building was restored by Hadrian in the second century CE. It has been used as a church since the fall of the Roman Empire and thus has survived pretty much intact. It contains the tombs of modern Italy's monarchs as well as that of the Renaissance artist Raphael.

Two famous temples crowned the Mōns Capitōlīnus. The ridge between the two temples was called the *arx* (citadel). The Temple of Iuppiter Optimus Maximus is labeled T. Iovis on the city plan. Iovis is the possessive of Iuppiter, and T. stands for *templum*. The other temple on the Mōns Capitōlīnus was dedicated to Iūno Monēta. You may have read a famous story about the sacred geese housed in Iūno's temple whose squawks once alerted the Romans to an enemy attack. "Monēta" is thought to be related both to the Latin word *moneo*, to warn, and to the English word money. The imperial mint was actually housed in the basement of the temple of Iūno Monēta.

It is interesting to note that although Roman custom usually forbade burial within the walls of a city, the emperor Augustus constructed a large circular mausoleum on the east side of the Tiberis. Similarly, Hadrian built a magnificent tomb for himself and his family on the west bank of the Tiber. In the fifth century CE the emperor Honorius incorporated the Tomb of Hadrian into the fortification that he built to extend the third century Aurelian Wall. Today Hadrian's Tomb is known as the Castel Sant'Angelo. During the Middle Ages the Castel Sant'Angelo served as a fortress for Vatican City. Today, the structure houses a museum of armaments.

EXERCISES

I. Highlight on the city plan:

    1. the seven hills (Mōns Capitōlīnus, Collis Quirīnālis, Collis Vīminālis, Mōns Esquilīnus, Mōns Caelius, Mōns Aventīnus, Mōns Palātīnus)

    2. Cloāca Maxima

    3. Subūra

    4. Tiberis

    5. Colossēum

    6. Circus Maximus

    7. Temple of Iuppiter Optimus Maximus (T. Iovis)

    8. Panthēon

II.   Respondē breviter Latīnē.

    1. Ubi Rōmānī bovēs emere et vendere poterant?

    2. Ubi Rōmānī ad mūnera (gladiatorial games) spectanda veniēbant?

CITY OF ROME: DISTRICTS AND LANDMARKS

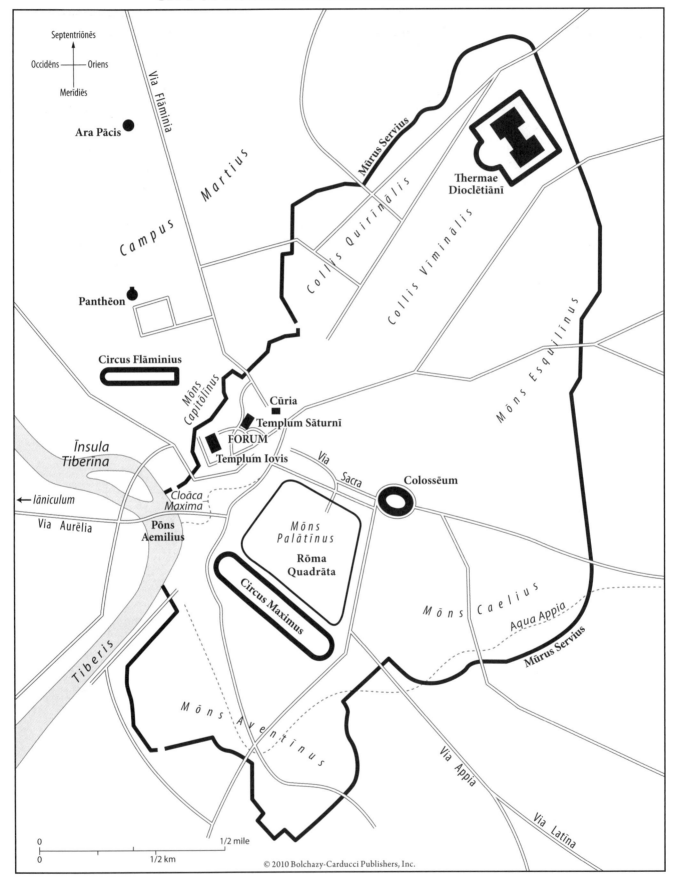

Septentriōnēs

Occidēns — Oriens

Meridiēs

Via Flāminia

Ara Pācis

Campus

Martius

Mūrus Servius

Thermae
Dioclētiānī

Collis Quirīnālis

Collis Vimīnālis

Panthēon

Mōns Esquilīnus

Circus Flāminius

*Mōns
Capitōlīnus*

Cūria

Templum Sāturnī

FORUM

Templum Iovis

Via
Sacra

Colossēum

Īnsula
Tiberīna

Cloāca
Maxima

← Iāniculum

Pōns
Aemilius

Via Aurēlia

*Mōns
Palātīnus*

Rōma
Quadrāta

Circus Maximus

Mōns Caelius

Aqua Appia

Mūrus Servius

Tiberis

Mōns Aventīnus

Via Appia

Via Latīna

0   1/2 mile

0   1/2 km

© 2010 Bolchazy-Carducci Publishers, Inc.

3. Quid est alterum nōmen Colossēī?

   _____

4. Ubi Rōmānī ad ludōs scaenicōs (theater productions) spectandōs veniēbant?

   _____

5. Quid est magnum templum dedicatum omnibus deīs deabusque?

   _____

6. Quis Domum Auream aedificāvit?

   _____

III. Īre ulterius

1. What is the Latin word for "golden"? What is the Latin word for "gold"? Where would you find the abbreviation "Au" used today?

   _____

   _____

2. Translate the name of this monument: _Ara Pācis._ Find out about the building. What does it look like? Who built it? Where was it located? When was it rediscovered and restored?

   _____

   _____

   _____

   _____

3. Translate the phrase _Forma Urbis._ What is it? How does it help archeologists determine the size and location of vanished structures in Rome?

   _____

   _____

   _____

   _____

4. Think about the word "Pantheon." Why was the famous temple given this name? What is the term for the hole in its dome? What role did the natural light coming from the dome play?

_____

_____

_____

5. Find a dotted line on the city plan marked Aqua Appia. Find out more about the aqueducts that supplied fresh water to the city of Rome. How many aqueducts served the city? From what sources did the aqueducts draw their water?

_____

_____

_____

6. In 1933 archaeologists began to construct a huge model of the city of Rome as it was in the fourth century CE. The model, called the Plastico di Roma Antica, can be seen today in the Museum of Roman civilization in the suburb of Rome called EUR. Use Google Images to find pictures of the model and locate as many landmarks of the city as you can. Find out what the abbreviation EUR stands for. Name the dictator who was in power in Italy in 1933. Why did he encourage archeologists to study the history of Rome?

_____

_____

_____

7. Use Google Images to find pictures of the two temples near the Tiber: the Temple of Portunus and the Temple of Hercules Olivarius. Describe each.

_____

_____

_____

_____

8. What is the inscription on the Pantheon? Translate it.

_____

_____

9. Visit Google Earth to see the ancient monuments of Rome in vivid three-dimensional reconstructions. http://sites.google.com/site/3dancientrome/

CITY OF ROME: DISTRICTS AND LANDMARKS

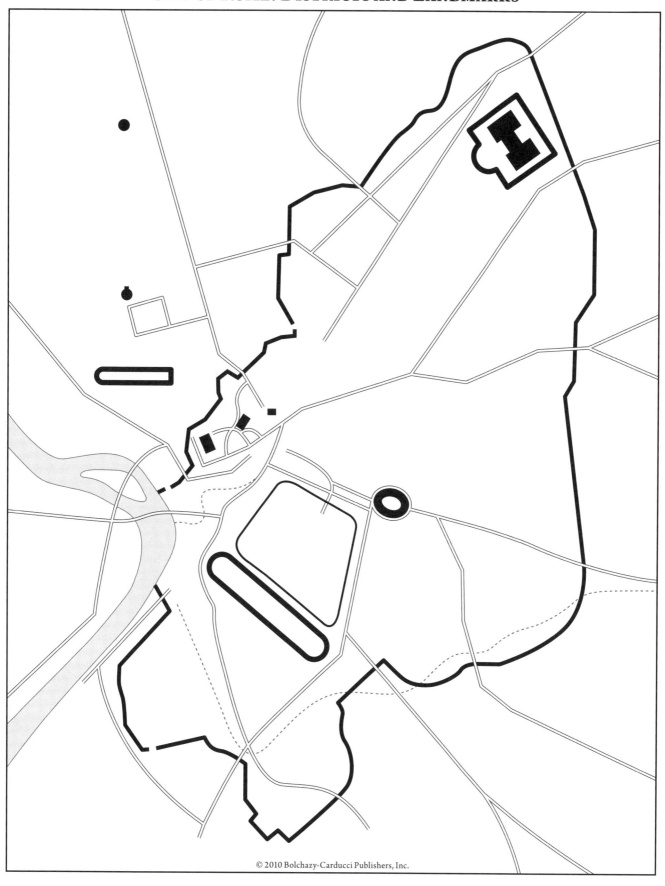

IV.   Test yourself! Label the blank map with the following:

1. Mōns Caelius
2. Collis Quirīnālis
3. Collis Vīminālis
4. Mōns Capitōlīnus
5. Mōns Aventīnus
6. Mōns Palātīnus
7. Tiberis
8. Īnsula Tiberīna

9. Forum
10. Cloāca Maxima
11. Subūra
12. Colossēum
13. Circus Maximus
14. Temple of Iuppiter Optimus Maximus
15. Panthēon
16. Campus Martius

TRANSLATION OF EXERCISE II

Respondē breviter Latīnē = Answer briefly in Latin.

1. Ubi Rōmānī bovēs emere et vendere poterant? = Where were the Romans able to buy and sell cows?

2. Ubi Rōmānī ad mūnera (gladiatorial games) spectanda veniēbant? = Where did the Romans come to watch gladiatorial games?

3. Quid est alterum nōmen Colossēī? = What is another name of the Colosseum?

4. Ubi Rōmānī ad ludōs scaenicōs (theater productions) spectandōs veniēbant? = Where did the Romans go to watch theater productions?

5. Quid est magnum templum dedicatum omnibus deīs deabusque? = What is the big temple dedicated to all the gods and goddesses?

6. Quis Domum Auream aedificāvit? = Who built the Golden House?

The Forum/Forum Rōmānum

The Forum Rōmānum lies between the Mōns Palātīnus and the Mōns Capitōlīnus (at the western end of the plan). It was the site of several of the city's oldest and most important temples. It was also home to the major law courts and the Senate House. In addition, the Forum served as a museum. In fact, so many statues and monuments eventually filled the space that during the Empire additional fora were created in adjoining areas by Augustus, Vespasian, Nerva, and Trajan.

When a Roman entered the Forum on the Via Sacra (Sacred Way), he would climb the gentle slope of the Velia, a spur of the Palatine Hill. Here, the Arch of Titus, which commemorated Titus's victory over Jerusalem in 70 CE, provides an impressive entrance to the Forum. Note the nearby "Templum Jovis Statōris," where the Senate was meeting when Cicero denounced Catiline. The Templum Veneris et Rōmae was the largest and most splendid in the Roman world with a double apse designed by the emperor Hadrian himself. Find the Via Sacra on the plan of the Forum. Now, locate the round Templum Vestae (Temple of Vesta), where an eternal flame burned. Next, notice the Ātrium Vestae (House of the Vestals). This was home to the six Vestal Virgins who tended Vesta's sacred fire. Just beyond the Ātrium Vestae you can see the Templum Castoris (Temple of Castor). Castor and his twin brother Pollux, known together as the Geminī, were minor gods who were especially dear to the Romans. At the foot of the Mōns Capitōlīnus, you can see the Templum Sāturnī (Temple to Saturn), another large and important temple. In the basement of the Temple to Saturn was the city's *aerārium* (treasury) where gold and silver bullion was stored. Saturn is another name for Cronus, the Titan whose reign is associated in mythology with a Golden Age. The side of the Mōns Capitōlīnus overlooking the forum housed the Tabulārium, where records including the plans of Roman cities were stored.

The Forum housed three law courts. The Basilica of Constantine is the newest. It was so large that the French cavalry used it for a riding ring when Napoleon occupied Rome. You can find the oldest law court, the Basilica Iūlia, between the Temple of Castor and the Temple of Saturn. The third of the Forum law courts is the Basilica Aemilia next to the Cūria (Senate House). It is interesting that early Christians copied the floor plan of Roman basilicas when they were designing church buildings to accommodate large groups of people. The center section of a church or cathedral came to be called the nave because it resembled the interior of a Roman *nāvis* (ship). While the entrance to the Roman basilica was through an entrance on the long side, the entrance to the Christian basilica was from the short end. Thus, for those entering the orientation drew the worshipper's eyes directly down the central aisle, the nave, to the altar.

Notice how small the Cūria is in comparison to any of the three basilicas. As today major urban areas regularly undergo renovations and changes. This plan shows such a change by marking the location of the earlier Cūria Hostīlia and the Comitium as well as the later Cūria Iūlia. The present building, converted to a church, is a much later version from Diocletian's reign. Speeches could be delivered to a crowd from the outdoor rostra (speaker's platform). You can see that the rostra is quite close to the Cūria. It lies between the Arch of Septimius Sevērus and the Temple of Saturn. At one end of the rostra stood the *milliārium aureum*, the golden milestone, the marker to which all roads were considered to lead. The rostra itself was decorated with the beaks of those ships defeated by the Roman navy in the sea battle of Antium (Anzio) in 338 BCE. The Latin word for beak is *rostrum*. Hence, the structure's name.

It is interesting to note that when Augustus became the sole ruler of the Roman world, he built a temple to his adopted father Iūlius Caesar opposite the rostra. This Templum Dīvī Iūlī (Temple of the Divine Julius) stood between the Basilica Aemilia and the Temple of Castor. A flight of stairs led to a platform where speakers could stand to address a crowd. Augustus decorated his new speaker's platform with the beaks of the ships his forces had defeated at the battle of Actium. These two speaker's platforms of different eras provide a visible link between Augustus and his predecessors. They reflect the continuum of Roman history from Antium to Actium.

In the open area just in front of the Templum Dīvī Iūlī, you can see the Columna Phōcadis (Column of Phōcas), the last monument erected in the Forum. It was set up in 602 CE in honor of the Byzantine emperor Phōcas. By the time of Phōcas, the Roman Empire had long been divided, and the center of power was no longer Rome, but rather Constantīnopolis in the east. Fittingly, the Column of Phōcas is made up of several different elements scavenged from other buildings. In fact, many of the buildings and monuments in the Forum were destroyed through the centuries when materials were taken from them for new buildings. On the other hand, some of the ancient buildings were adapted to other uses. The Temple of Antōninus and Faustīna, for example, became a church while the Arch of Titus became part of a palace belonging to the Frangipani family. Eventually, the Forum became overgrown, and the resulting wilderness was known as the Campo di Vaccino (the Cow Pasture).

EXERCISES

I.   Highlight the following on your Forum plan:

    1.   Templum Vestae (Temple of Vesta)

    2.   Ātrium Vestae (House of the Vestals)

    3.   Templum Castoris (Temple of Castor)

    4.   Templum Sāturnī (Temple of Saturn)

    5.   Templum Dīvī Iūlī (Temple of the Divine Julius)

    6.   Via Sacra (Sacred Way)

    7.   Basilica Iūlia

    8.   Basilica Aemilia

    9.   Cūria

    10.   Rostra

    11.   Columna Phōcadis (column of Phōcas)

    12.   Arcus Augustī

    13.   "Templum Jovis Statōris"

    14.   Basilica Constantīnī

II.   Respondē breviter Latīnē.

    1.   Quot Virginēs Vestālēs erant?

    _____

    2.   Quī deus erat frater Castoris?

    _____

    3.   Ubi erat aerārium urbis Rōmae?

    _____

City of Rome: Forum Rōmānum

1 Tabulārium
2 Porticus Deōrum Consentium
3 Templum Vespāsiānī
4 Templum Concordiae
5 Templum Saturnī
6 Mīliārium Aureum
7 Umbilīcus Urbis
8 Rostra
9 Arcus Septimiī Sevērī
10 Lapis Niger
11 Comitium
12 Cūria Hostīlia
13 Cūria Iūlia
14 Basilica Iūlia
15 Columna Phōcadis
16 Lacus Curtius
17 Fanum Iānī Geminī
18 Templum Castoris et Pollūcis
19 Porticus Gāiī et Lūciī
20 Basilica Aemilia
21 Arcus Augustī
22 Fanum et Lacus Iūturnae
23 Templum Dīvī Iūliī
24 Templum Vestae
25 Domus Vestālium
26 Domus Pontificis Maximī
27 Rēgia
28 Templum Antōnīnī et Faustīnae
29 "Templum Rōmulī"
30 mansiōnēs*
31 Basilica Constantīnī
32 Arcus Titī
33 "Templum Iovis Statōris"
34 Templum Veneris et Rōmae

*from Republican era
NB: Quotation marks around a building
indicate that its identity or location is
not definitive.

III. Īre ulterius

1. What do the bas-reliefs inside the Arch of Titus illustrate? Describe those on the two inner spaces of the arch.

   _____

   _____

   _____

2. What is the believed function of the building labeled as the Rēgia on the Forum Plan?

   _____

   _____

   _____

3. What Italian engraver is famous for his depictions of the ruins of Rome and the Campo Vaccino? Find several examples of his engravings. How is each of your choices representative of a contemporary appearance of the ruins? Explain with details.

   _____

   _____

   _____

   _____

4. Find out more about the Lapis Niger, the Tomb of Rōmulus, the Umbilicus, and the Lacus Curtius.

   _____

   _____

   _____

   _____

5. What are some of the ways scholars have been able to find out what the Forum looked like at different periods of Roman history? How did they discover information on specific buildings like the Temple of Vesta in order to restore it accurately? How do they know what the Temple of Iānus or the Arch of Augustus looked like since they have completely disappeared?

   _____

   _____

   _____

   _____

6. Use Google Images to find an image of the Temple of Antōninus and Faustīna. What aspect of the building clearly shows the changed ground level of the Forum?

_____

_____

_____

_____

7. Investigate the changes to the Forum made during the reign of Augustus and delineate the major ones.

_____

_____

_____

_____

IV. Test yourself! Label the blank map of the Forum with the following:

1. Templum Vestae (Temple of Vesta)

2. Ātrium Vestae (House of the Vestals)

3. Templum Castoris (Temple of Castor)

4. Templum Sāturnī (Temple of Saturn)

5. Via Sacra (Sacred Way)

6. Basilica Iūlia

7. Basilica Aemilia

8. Cūria

9. Rostra

10. Columna Phōcadis (column of Phōcas)

V. City of Rome Projects

1. Relief Map of the City

Use quick-drying clay or papier-mâché to show the hills of Rome. Label the hills, the Tiberis, the Īnsula Tiberīna, the Forum, the Iāniculum, and the boundaries of Rōma Quadrāta. Be sure to include a compass rose.

2. Research each of the buildings marked on the map. Find out when and under whose patronage they were built. Discuss 2–3 significant facts about each building.

NB: For this assignment, each student can be assigned a building or buildings depending on class size and then each would give a mini-presentation to the class using PowerPoint™ or a similar format.

City of Rome: Forum Rōmānum

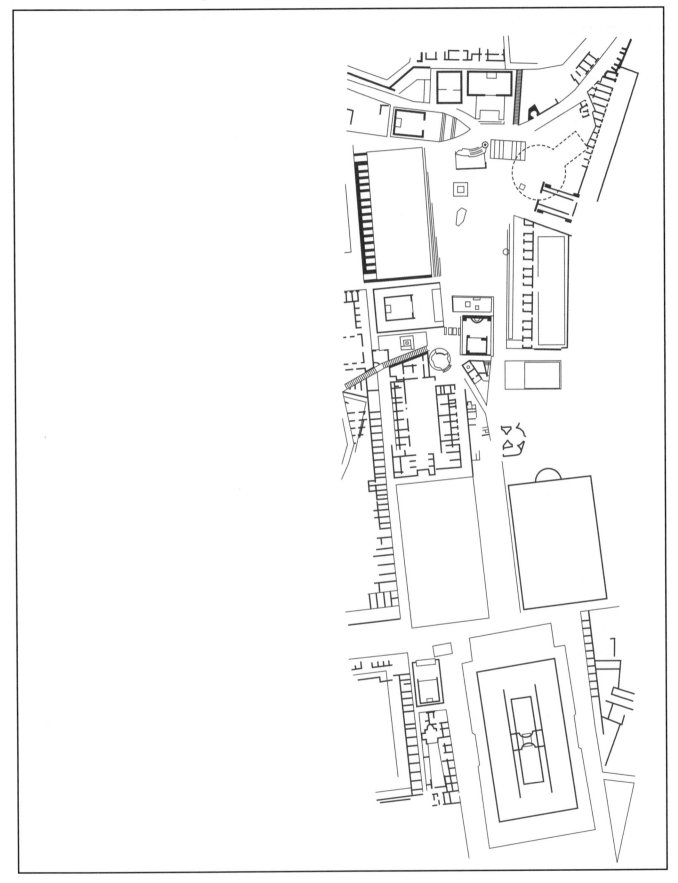

3. Posters

   Pick one of the following subjects. Print images from the Internet, or make sketches of your own to arrange on a poster for your classroom.

   - the Colossēum

   - the Panthēon

   - the Circus Maximus

   - three (3) triumphal arches: Titus, Constantine, Septimius Severus

   - two (2) columns: Marcus Aurelius and Trajan

   - walls and gates of ancient Rome

   - the tomb of Augustus and the Castel Sant'Angelo

   - other buildings worldwide whose domes were influenced by the dome of the Panthēon (e.g., the Capitol in Washington, St. Peter's in Rome, St. Paul's in London, the Pantheon in Paris, the Rotunda at the University of Virginia). Be sure to include any buildings in your hometown that have Roman-inspired domes.

4. Domus Aurea Report

   Give a five-minute oral summary on the recent news reports of the excavation of Nero's Golden House such as the article from the *New York Times* available at http://www.nytimes.com/1999/06/25/style/25iht-trdomus.2.t.html.

Translation of Exercise II

Respondē breviter Latīnē = Answer briefly in Latin.

1. Quot Virginēs Vestālēs erant? = How many Vestal Virgins were there?

2. Quī deus erat frater Castoris? = Which god was the brother of Castor?

3. Ubi erat aerārium urbis Rōmae? = Where was the treasury of the city of Rome?

V. Sinus Cūmānus
The Bay of Naples

You probably remember from your earlier study of the Italian peninsula that colonists from Greece played an important role in the culture of southern Italy and Sicily, and that the whole region was known as Magna Graecia. You may also know that settlers from the Greek island of Euboea established the colony of Cūmae at the north end of the Sinus Cūmānus (the Bay of Naples) in the eighth century BCE.

The people of Cūmae founded a city called Parthenope near the midpoint of the Sinus Cūmānus. Subsequently they established the port of Neāpolis (Naples) adjacent to Parthenope. The two towns eventually grew together into a single bustling seaport known as Neāpolis. The city of Neāpolis became an ally of Rome and the capital of the region called Campānia. The Romans knew the area as *Fēlix Campānia* because *fēlix* in Latin means fertile, productive, happy, or lucky. Campānia was indeed extremely fertile. It produced fruit, flowers, and wine in abundance. One of the reasons for the productivity of the region undoubtedly has to do with the richness of soil created from volcanic material.

Vesuvius Mōns lies to the east of Neāpolis. It is part of a chain of volcanoes that stretches from Tuscany, in Northern Italy, all the way south to Sicily and the Lipari Islands of Aeolia and Vulcānia. Most of the other volcanoes in the chain, except for Aetna Mōns in Sicily, are extinct, but Vesuvius is only dormant.

The whole area around the Sinus Cūmānus (Bay of Naples) is still bedeviled by volcanic activity. For example, the ground level of the town of Puteolī (Pozzuoli) southeast of Lacus Avernus is constantly rising because of underlying volcanic pressure. The district north of Puteolī, the Campī Phlegraeī (Phlegrian Fields), is filled with hot springs and craters that emit steam and hot gas. The area is a hellish landscape of hot bubbling mud pools.

The Romans believed that the entrance to the Underworld lay near Cūmae. When you read Vergil's *Aeneid*, you will learn know that Book 6 begins with Aeneas's visit to the Temple of Apollo at Cūmae. Here, he is able to consult the Cumaean Sibyl, Apollo's priestess and prophet. The Sibyl acts as Aeneas's guide as he visits his father Anchises in the Underworld. To find the entrance to the Underworld Aeneas follows two doves sent by his mother Venus. The birds leave him at the edge of Lake Avernus because according to tradition, birds always avoided the smelly, sulfurous fumes of the lake. You can see both Cūmae and Lacus Avernus west of Neāpolis.

The ancient inhabitants of Campānia seem to have been largely unaware of Vesuvius's lethal potential. Not long before the famous eruption of 79 CE, the Greek geographer Strabo had observed that the cindery stones near the summit looked "eaten out by fires," (*Geography* 5.4.8) but he did not seem to realize that Vesuvius might soon erupt. The crater of Vesuvius was not visible from below so perhaps it is not surprising that the mountain seemed only a benign presence looming over the rich agricultural region around the Bay of Naples. Indeed, Bāiae, just south of Cūmae, and Herculāneum, near Neāpolis, were popular resort towns. Pompēiī was a business center and a seaport although you will notice that it is no longer on the sea because the coastline changed with the eruption of Vesuvius. Stabiae, a small town, which you can find south of Pompēiī, was surrounded by elegant villas belonging to prosperous Romans. The emperor Tiberius spent the last years of his life on the island of Capreae (Capri), which lies in the Sinus Cūmānus, just east of the peninsula of Surrentum (Sorrento). Tiberius built several elegant villas on Capreae, each with breathtaking views of the sea and of the rocky coastline across the bay.

Vesuvius gave a warning of its true nature in 62 CE, when a serious earthquake caused significant damage to many buildings in Pompēiī. No one, however, seems to have realized that this earthquake was an indication that a major eruption might soon follow. Seventeen years later, in the early summer of 79 CE, while major rebuilding from the earthquake was still going on, many wells around Pompēiī dried up. With hindsight, volcanologists can see that the drying up of the wells was a result of the movement of the earth's tectonic plates. When the plate on which Africa rests collided with the European plate, its edge began to slide down, becoming more and more unstable and beginning to melt. Pools of molten rock called magma were pushed toward the earth's surface. Increasing pressure from below finally awoke Vesuvius from its long sleep.

As Vesuvius erupted, the magma poured forth both as ash and as lava. Vesuvius emitted enough ashes to fill a cube 1.5 miles on each side. The flow of hot ash was followed by a second kind of ash deposit called an ignimbrite, which, moving at high speed, forms a layer of tightly compacted ash. As the ash flow released more magma, the central part of the volcano collapsed. The hole that is left is called the *caldera*, from the Spanish word for kettle that, in turn, comes from the Latin *caldus*, meaning warm. If a volcano is on an island like the Greek island of ancient Thēra (Santorini), the formation of the caldera can cause a huge tidal wave. The tidal wave that followed the volcanic explosion on Thēra, around 1400 BCE, destroyed much of the Aegean civilization on the northern section of Crete. Vesuvius is not on an island so no tidal wave followed, but Monte Somma, the original cone of the volcano, bears a huge depression.

After the cataclysm of 79, Vesuvius erupted nine more times in the next thousand years. A major eruption in 1139 was followed by 500 years of quiet. Another major eruption occurred in 1631, and since then there have been eruptions every 35 or 40 years. In recent times, Vesuvius stirred in 1944 during the Second World War, and this eruption was captured on film by the allied armies. Today an observatory on Vesuvius tracks seismic activity. While a series of small earthquakes in 1980 were not followed by an eruption, Vesuvius is a continuing malevolent presence brooding over the Campanian landscape.

The sheer horror of Vesuvius's violence comes alive across the centuries in an eyewitness account of the eruption by the Roman author Pliny the Younger (61–114 BCE). Long after the disaster, the historian Tacitus asked Pliny to tell him about the eruption. Pliny was only eighteen at the time of the eruption, but he had searing memories of the terrifying savagery of Vesuvius, in part because his own uncle and adopted father, Pliny the Elder (23–79 BCE), perished in the aftermath of the eruption.

In his first letter to Tacitus, Pliny the Younger says that at the time of the eruption his uncle was serving as the admiral of the Roman fleet stationed at Mīsēnum on the northern side of the Bay of Naples. Admiral Pliny, who was interested in all sorts of natural phenomena and had written a 37-volume compendium of scientific lore called the *Natural Histories*, was eager to examine the smoking mountain at close quarters. His nephew, however, says that he did not accompany the expedition himself because he was busy doing a homework assignment. There were earth tremors but these, as young Pliny remarks, were so common in the area that no one paid them any attention. Apparently, even Pliny the Elder did not realize the magnitude of the disaster at first. In fact, on the morning of August 24, he was not sure which mountain was emitting the first plumes of smoke. He mistakenly thought that the cloud was sent up by a strong gust of wind from the mountain rather than from the tremendous pressure of the erupting volcano. Just as he was preparing to have a boat launched, a message arrived from a friend whose escape by land had been cut off. The admiral immediately set out on a mission of rescue instead of one of scientific inquiry. The sea was incredibly rough and the air was full of ash and little pumice stones called *lapilli*. The pilot begged to turn back, but Pliny the Elder insisted that they press on to his friend's house at a coastal town of Stabiae. There, he calmly had a meal, bathed, and took a nap. When the courtyard of the house began to fill with ash, his companions woke him. They debated whether to stay inside, risking the collapse of walls and roof, or whether to venture onto the shore where *lapilli* were raining like hail. Covering their heads with pillows, the group finally made its way outside. Pliny the Elder inhaled the sulphurous fumes and suffocated there on the beach.

Volcanologists have studied Pliny the Younger's letter to Tacitus, and Pliny the Elder would probably be pleased that the first phase of an explosive volcanic eruption has been given the name "Plinian Phase." The letter describes the cloud that rose from Vesuvius as resembling an umbrella pine, the Roman pine, a tree with a long trunk and spreading branches. A volcanic eruption does indeed produce a mushroom-shaped cloud similar to that associated with a nuclear explosion.

In some ways, Pliny the Younger's second letter to Tacitus about the eruption is even more frightening than the first. In the second letter, he describes the terrifying darkness that blocked the sun. He says that the darkness was not like darkness at night, in which objects can be dimly discerned, but like the darkness of an enclosed room. He depicts the panic and disorientation experienced by hundreds of fleeing people as they tried to escape from the affected area. Children were separated from their parents. Husbands and wives lost each other. Their cries were drowned by the rumble of thunder. Lightning flashed. Floors buckled. Buildings trembled and collapsed, blocking familiar roads. The earth tremors were so violent that vehicles were constantly thrown from one side of the road to the other, making it almost impossible to make progress. Even when the carts were loaded with stones whose weight should have acted as ballast and kept the carts upright, the roads were impassable. Pliny the Younger and his mother stumbled along on foot until his mother begged him to go on without her. He refused to leave her and, holding her by the hand so that they would not be separated, they struggled back to Mīsēnum to await the dawn.

The emperor Titus sent aid to the stricken communities and gradually, as the survivors of the disaster rebuilt their homes and their lives, memories of the Vesuvian cities and of the eruption grew dim. Ironically, the deaths of Pompeii and Herculaneum were to assure their immortality.

EXERCISES

I.   Highlight the following on the map:

1. Sinus Cūmānus

2. Capreae

3. Cūmae

4. Mīsēnum

5. Lacus Avernus

6. Campī Phlegraeī

7. Puteolī

8. Bāiae

9. Neāpolis

10. Vesuvius Mōns

11. Herculāneum

12. Pompēiī

13. Stabiae

14. Surrentum

BAY OF NAPLES

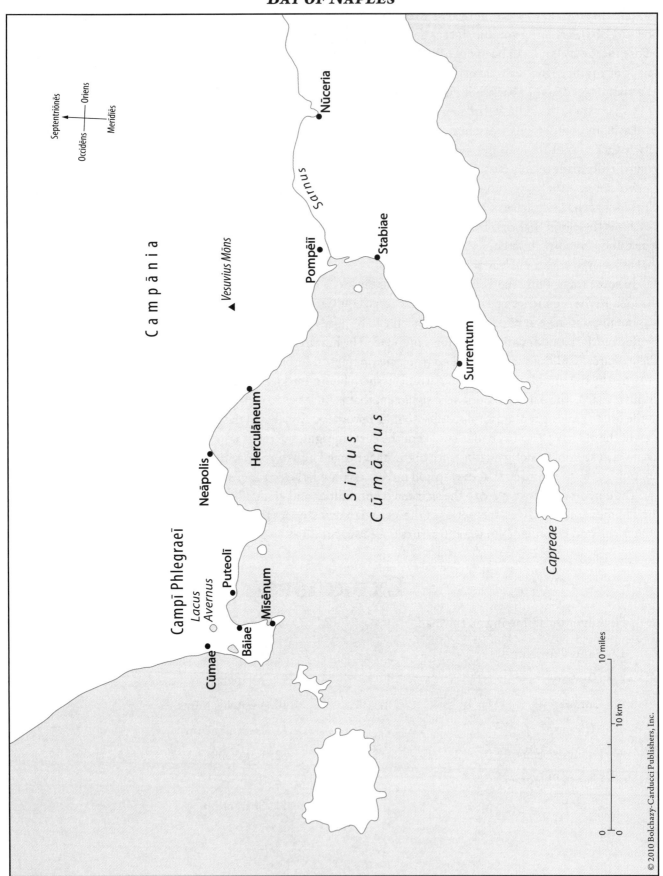

Septentriōnēs

Occidēns —— Oriēns

Merīdiēs

C a m p ā n i a

Nūceria

▲ Vesuvius Mōns

Pompēiī

Sarnus

Stabiae

Herculāneum

Surrentum

Neāpolis

S i n u s

C ū m ā n u s

Campī Phlegraeī

Lacus

Avernus

Puteolī

Misēnum

Bāiae

Cūmae

Capreae

10 miles

10 km

II. Match the ancient names to the modern ones:

1. _____ Surrentum   A. Naples

2. _____ Sinus Cūmānus   B. Phlegraean Fields

3. _____ Capreae   C. Pozzuoli

4. _____ Herculaneum   D. Capri

5. _____ Puteolī   E. Ercolano

6. _____ Campī Phlegraeī   F. Sorrento

7. _____ Neāpolis   G. Bay of Naples

III. Respondē breviter Latīnē.

1. Ubi est īnsula Euboeae?

    _____

2. Quī imperator Rōmānus rēgiās (palaces) Capreīs aedificāvit?

    _____

3. Quī auctor Rōmānus dē exitiō (destruction) Pompēiōrum scrīpsit?

    _____

IV. Īre ulterius

1. Find the town of Nūceria on the map. What happened when people from Nūceria rioted in the amphitheater at Pompēiī?

    _____

    _____

    _____

2. What was the *magnum opus* of Pliny the Elder? Read in translation a small portion of the work and give your reaction to what you have read.

    _____

    _____

    _____

3. Visit a tourist web site or consult a travel guide for the island of Capri. Then, write a brief description of the Blue Grotto.

_____

_____

_____

4. Visit a tourist web site or consult a travel guide for the Sorrentine Peninsula. Write a brief description of the famed Amalfi Drive.

_____

_____

_____

5. What were the Sibylline Books? What king of Rome is said to have foolishly destroyed some of the books?

_____

_____

_____

6. Find a photograph of what tradition identifies as the Sibyl's cavern at Cūmae. Write a brief description.

_____

_____

_____

7. Read in translation (or in Latin!) the two letters (_Epistulae_ 6.16 and 20) by Pliny the Younger to the historian Tacitus describing the eruption of Vesuvius. What strikes you most about this first person account of the disaster?

_____

_____

_____

8. What two Greek words make up the name of Neāpolis? What does each word mean? What are some examples of names of other cities that end in "polis"?

_____

_____

_____

Bay of Naples

V.   Test yourself! Label the blank map with the following:

1. Sinus Cūmānus (Bay of Naples)
2. Capreae (Capri)
3. Cūmae
4. Mīsēnum
5. Lacus Avernus
6. Campī Phlegraeī (Phlegrian Fields)
7. Puteolī (Pozzuoli)
8. Baīae
9. Neāpolis (Naples)
10. Vesuvius Mōns
11. Herculāneum
12. Pompēiī
13. Stabiae
14. Surrentum (Sorrento)

TRANSLATION OF EXERCISE III

Respondē breviter Latīnē = Answer briefly in Latin.

1. Ubi est īnsula Euboeae? = Where is the island of Euboea?

2. Quī imperator Rōmānus rēgiās (palaces) Capreīs aedificāvit? = What Roman emperor built palaces on Capri?

3. Quī auctor Rōmānus dē exitiō (destruction) Pompēiōrum scrīpsit? = What Roman author wrote about the destruction of Pompeii?

VI. Pompēiī
Pompeii

As you know from the previous chapter, 79 CE was a pivotal date for the whole area around the Bay of Naples, especially the city of Pompēiī. It was midday on August 24, 79 CE, when Mount Vesuvius erupted for the first time since the Bronze Age. It cast a column of ash and pumice 17 miles into the sky. The cloud of ash blotted out the sun. Six miles southeast of the volcano, the busy market town of Pompēiī was buried in a matter of hours as the cloud dropped a blanket of ash and pumice more than 15 feet deep. Small volcanic rocks, called *lapilli,* fell like hailstones. Violent waves prevented rescue from the sea.

After the disaster in 79, Pompēiī lay forgotten and undisturbed, covered by its shroud of ashes until the sixteenth century. In 1594 an engineer named Domenico Fontana, seeking to rechannel the water of the River Sarno, came upon some buildings in Pompēiī and an inscription with the word *decuriō Pompēiīs* (city official in Pompeii). He thought he had found a villa belonging to Caesar's contemporary, Pompey the Great. Much later, in 1748, Charles III, the Bourbon King of Naples, financed the first excavation of Pompēiī.

In the nineteenth century, after the Bourbon kings lost their hold on Naples, more systematic excavation was possible. The great nineteenth-century archaeologist Giuseppe Fiorelli developed a method of pouring plaster of paris into the hollows of the hardened volcanic material. The plaster takes on the shape of whatever was entombed in the ash, thus revealing the victims of the disaster in incredible detail.

Fiorelli is also responsible for another major contribution to Pompeian archaeology. As treasure seeking gave way to organized and systematic excavation, it was imperative for scholars to have a logical and consistent way of referring to streets and buildings. This posed a problem because the ancient inhabitants of Pompēiī did not give names to their streets or numbers to their buildings. An address might be given in general terms: *ad fullōnēs,* for example, meant in the cloth processors' district. Shops were sometimes identified by a painted sign or a stone bas-relief, but never with a number. Under Fiorelli's guidance, therefore, names were assigned to streets. Often, the name simply reflected the street's location. You can see that the street leading out of the corner of the Forum was called the Via del Foro. In other instances, a street was given a name based on one of its interesting features. The main street of Pompēiī was called the Via dell'Abbondanza because a fountain at one end of the street has a bas-relief of Ceres, the goddess of agriculture and abundant crops. Similarly, the Via del Mercurio was named for a bas-relief of the god Mercury on another fountain. Some streets were named after the towns to which they led. For example, the Via di Nola led through the Porta di Nōla to the town of Nōla, which was located about 15 miles to the east of Pompēiī.

Fiorelli usually called houses in Pompēiī by the name of their owners if this could be determined. The Domus Vettiōrum (House of the Vettii), for example, is named for the two brothers who were living there at the time of the eruption of Vesuvius. If the owners were not known, Fiorelli often chose a name that referred to a notable painting or an unusual artifact found in the individual house. Thus, the Domus Faunī (House of the Faun) takes its name from a small bronze statue of a dancing faun found in the pool of the atrium of the house. The faun has the head and body of a man but the legs and hooves of a goat.

Fiorelli's team also divided Pompēiī into sections. Each *regiō*, or section, has a number. Within each *regiō* are *īnsulae* or blocks. You probably know the word *īnsula* in Latin as "island," but if you think of the streets of a town taking the place of a river, "block" also makes sense as a meaning. A single large house, such as the House of the Faun, may occupy an entire *īnsula*. Today, guidebooks and archaeologists identify specific houses by *regiō*, *īnsula*, and position within the *īnsula*. The House of Lūcius Caecilius Iūcundus, for example, is listed as *Reg. V, Īns.1, No. 26*.

A quick glance at the plan of Pompēiī reveals that in the eastern part of the city, near the amphitheater, the streets are laid out in a symmetrical grid pattern. This orderly system is typical of Roman city planning. As excavators uncovered the western section around the Forum, however, a twisting maze of streets came to light. These winding streets are a reminder of Pompēiī's past. They date from the early Greek settlement of the sixth century BCE or from an early period of domination by a native Italian tribe called the Samnites. A few inscriptions in Oscan, a Samnite tongue, bear witness to this period in Pompēiī's history. In the Social War of 90–89, Pompēiī joined other Italian towns in a revolt against Rome. The Roman dictator Sulla put down the rebellion but later granted Pompēiī the status of a *mūnicipium*. This meant that its citizens had the rights of Roman citizens. Pompēiī grew into a prosperous trading center, home to several thriving industries, including cloth processing and fish sauce manufacture. Its population in 79 was close to 22,000.

Notice the walls as you look at the city plan. The whole city of Pompēiī was originally surrounded by a wall—actually two walls about 20 feet apart with the space between filled with rubble. Towers three stories high strengthened the fortification at its weakest points. The wall was breached by eight gates. Near the Porta Vesuvīna, damage done by the catapults of Sulla's army in the Social War is still visible. Another gate to note is the Porta Marīna. It had two openings, one for pedestrians and another for wheeled vehicles. Part of the southwestern wall was demolished during the peaceful days of the early empire. It was no longer needed for defense, and it blocked the sea view for the opulent houses in that part of town. Notice that tombs lie outside the walls in several locations, and remember that Roman burials were almost always outside of a city.

Inside the city walls, you can easily locate the amphitheater and the two theaters. As in Rome, the entertainment provided by gladiatorial games and theater productions was clearly an important part of daily life here. You can see that a *lūdus gladiātorius* (training school for gladiators) was conveniently located near the amphitheater. Also in this part of town, you will notice an extensive exercise ground labeled the *palaestra*. Wealthy young men would have played ball and exercised here. A smaller *palaestra*, patronized by men of more modest means, was actually inside the Stabian Baths. You should note that in addition to the Stabian Baths, there were two other public baths in the town. It is interesting to note that the design of both the bath complexes and of the amphitheater in Pompēiī was later replicated all over the Roman Empire.

The Forum of Pompēiī was the location of an impressive basilica where court cases were heard and the curia where the town council met. At one end of the Forum you can see the Temple of Iūppiter, which had been damaged in the earthquake of 62. Interestingly, it was still being repaired at the time of the eruption of Vesuvius, and was actually being used to store building materials. The Temple to Apollo and the Temple to Venus were apparently less seriously damaged in 62 and were in use at the time of the city's destruction.

Another temple that had been completely repaired and was clearly in use at the time of the eruption was the temple of Isis, located near the theaters. It is the best preserved of all the shrines in Pompēiī. Isis is a deity whose worship began in Egypt. Why were Pompeians attracted to the worship of an Egyptian goddess? Why was her temple repaired so promptly when Jupiter's temple was being used to store stone? What was Isis's appeal? The

Romans regularly incorporated foreign cults into their worship, and after the Second Punic War (241–210 BCE), the worship of Isis became popular in Rome. Isis, like her brother/husband Osiris, ruled in the Underworld. She decreed the fate of men, meting out punishments and rewards. Devotion to Isis promised a chance of eternal life.

On August 24, the priests of Isis were getting ready for lunch when the eruption occurred. They tried to save the sacred objects from the temple but one by one they were overcome by the poisonous fumes and suffocated. Plaster casts have been made of their bodies.

At the entrance to the Forum of Pompēiī, you will notice a building labeled the *Aedificium Eumachiae* (Building of Eumachia). Scholars think that this may have been a cloth market owned by a prominent business woman. Cloth processing was an important industry in Pompēiī, and you can find the *fullōnica* (cloth processing plant) of Verēcundus on the Via dell'Abbondanza. Other businesses to locate include the *Caupona Asellinae* (Inn of Asellina) and the *Pistrīnum Modestī* (Bakery of Modestus). Notice that there is no clear division between the business part of the town and the residential district. Many homes had shops at the front of the house. In fact, from the street, a passerby would not be able to discern the size or opulence of an individual house. The elaborate fountains, pools, gardens, sculptures, mosaics, and wall paintings within the houses of the prosperous inhabitants of Pompēiī would not have been visible at all.

EXERCISES

I.   Highlight on the city plan:

1. Templum Apollonis (Temple of Apollo)

2. Templum Veneris (Temple of Venus)

3. Templum Iōvis (Temple of Jupiter)

4. Templum Īsis (Temple of Isis)

5. Basilica (law court)

6. Forum

7. Aedificium Eumachiae (Building of Eumachia)

8. Thermae (Forum Baths)

9. Caupona Asellinae (Inn of Asellina)

10. Pistrīnum Modestī (Bakery of Modestus)

11. Domus Faunī (House of the Faun)

12. Domus Vettiōrum (House of the Vettii)

13. Domus Iūcundī (House of Iucundus)

14. Domus Menandrūs (House of Menander)

15. Theātrum (Theater)

16. Ōdēum (Odeon/music hall/small theater)

17. Amphitheātrum (amphitheater)

18. Palaestra (gymnasium/exercise ground)

19. Lūdus gladiātorius (gladiatorial barracks)

City of Pompeii

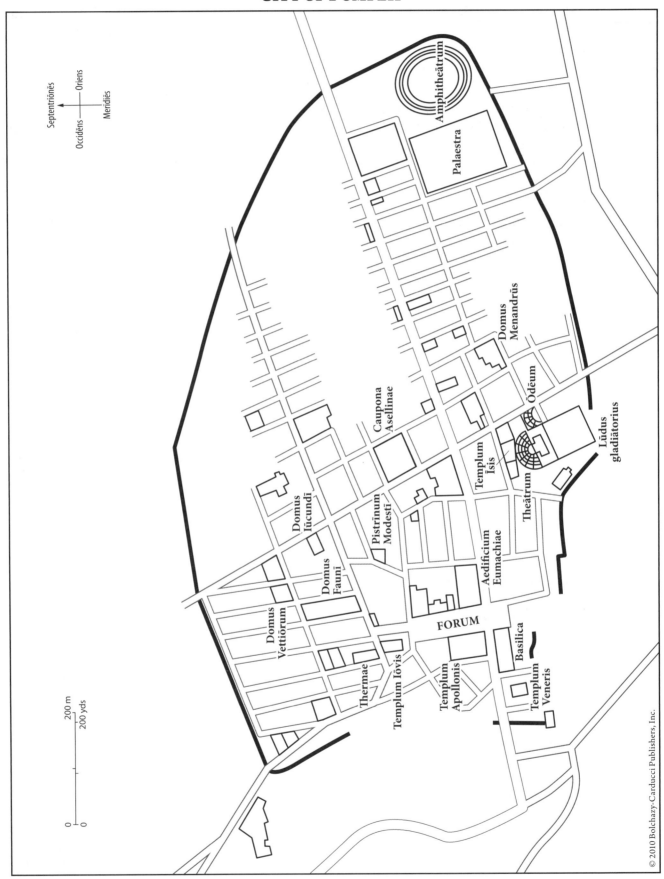

Septentriōnēs

Orīens

Occidēns

Merīdiēs

200 m

200 yds

0

0

Amphitheātrum

Palaestra

Domus
Menandrūs

Ōdēum

Caupona
Asellinae

Lūdus
gladiātorius

Templum
Īsis

Theātrum

Domus
Iūcundī

Pistrīnum
Modestī

Aedificium
Eumachiae

Domus
Faunī

Domus
Vettiōrum

FORUM

Basilica

Thermae

Templum Iōvis

Templum
Apollōnis

Templum
Veneris

II. Īre ulterius

1. Find a picture of the bust of Lūcius Caecilius Iūcundus that was found in the ātrium of the House of Iūcundus. Describe Iūcundus.

   _____

   _____

   _____

2. Many of the surviving graffiti in Pompēiī are slogans urging people to vote for particular candidates. Find and translate three examples of this type of graffito.

   _____

   _____

   _____

3. Locate the Villa of Mysteries on your plan of Pompēiī. Find out why its name is appropriate.

   _____

   _____

   _____

4. Find out the origin of the name of the House of the Silver Wedding.

   _____

   _____

   _____

III. Pompēiī Projects

1. Find out about one of the other archeological sites on the Bay of Naples. Stabiae, Herculāneum, Oplontis, and Boscoreale are all well documented. Write a brief report. Be sure to list your sources.

2. Choose one public building in Pompēiī, e.g., the basilica, and prepare a poster with images of both the exterior and the interior. Include a floor plan and a description of the daily activities that would have taken place there. Be sure to list your sources.

3. Pick a private house in Pompēiī and prepare a poster with images of both the exterior and the interior. Be sure to list your sources.

4. Make a copy of a mosaic from Pompēiī. Use candy, bits of colored paper, or fish gravel for the _tesserae_. Painted egg shell is another medium that can be used in mosaic work. You might want to recreate a whole panel such as the famous _Cave Canem_ mosaic, or you might choose to reproduce only a part of a larger mosaic.

CITY OF POMPEII

VII. Historia Rōmāna
Roman History

Part I: Conquest of the Italian Peninsula

The traditional date for the founding of Rome is 753 BCE, and if you are a Latin student, you probably know the legend of Romulus and Remus, the twin sons of the god Mars, who were left as infants to die on the bank of the Tiber. Nursed by a mother wolf, and later adopted by a shepherd and his wife, the twins grew up and began to build rival cities. Then, according to the story, Romulus killed his brother in a dispute over which city had the bigger fortifications. Romulus's city was, of course, the city of Rome, and Romulus was the first king of Rome.

Like so many other stories of Rome's early days, the tale of the twins clearly belongs to the realm of myth and legend. Sometimes, however, the legends are supported by historical evidence. For example, scholars agree that in the seventh century BCE, Rome came in contact with the Etruscans, a highly civilized people of northern Italy; indeed, according to the Roman historian Livy, two of the later kings of Rome were of Etruscan origin. You can see on the map the Etruscan stronghold of Vēiī, in the region called Etrūria less than twenty miles from Rome. The Etruscan alphabet and language have never been fully deciphered, but much has been learned about Etruscan culture from artifacts and paintings found in their tombs.

In 390 BCE, Rome was attacked and burned by the Gauls, a fierce northern tribe. The records of the early history of the city perished in the fire, but the Romans finally managed to drive the Gauls back to northern Italy beyond the Padus (Po) River. This part of Italy came to be known as Gallia Cisalpīna (Cisalpine Gaul) i.e., Gaul on the near (to Rome) side of the Alps.

Later in the fourth century BCE, the Romans faced another enemy. This time, their foe was a ferocious tribe native to central Italy called the Samnites. The Roman army suffered a major defeat at the hands of the Samnites at the battle of the Furculae Caudīnae (Caudine Forks) in 321 BCE, but eventually the Romans managed to subdue the Samnites, who became their allies.

Meanwhile, the Greek settlers in Sicily and southern Italy had grown prosperous, and they viewed Rome's increasing power with trepidation. In 282 BCE, Tarentum, a Greek colony in southern Italy, sought reinforcements from Greece in a dispute with Rome. The Greek army was under the command of a general from Ēpīrus named Pyrrhus. The Greek army of invasion was especially formidable because Pyrrhus had introduced the elephant as a military instrument in this campaign. The Greeks defeated the Roman army at Hēraclēa in 280 BCE, and again at Asculum in 279 BCE. In both battles, the Romans lost more men than the Greeks, but Pyrrhus knew that the Romans had many more men that they could recruit as reinforcements. In 275 BCE after the battle of Beneventum, Pyrrhus is supposed to have said that one more such victory would utterly undo him. You may have heard the expression, a pyrrhic victory, meaning an empty or technical win. After this last battle, Pyrrhus returned to Greece, leaving Rome in control of the entire Italian peninsula.

EXERCISES

I.   Highlight on your map:

1. Etrūria

2. Vēiī

3. Gallia Cisalpīna (Cisalpine Gaul)

4. Samnium

5. Furculae Caudīnae (Caudine Forks)

6. Tarentum (Taranto)

II.   Respondē breviter Latīnē.

1. Quī Vēiīs habitābant?

_____

2. Cur Rōmānī tabulās historiae suae non habuērunt?

_____

3. Quis erat Pyrrhus?

_____

III. Īre ulterius

1. Find out more about the Etruscans. Describe the Etruscan tombs found in Cerverteri and Tarquinia.

_____

_____

_____

_____

ROMAN HISTORY: CONQUEST OF ITALY

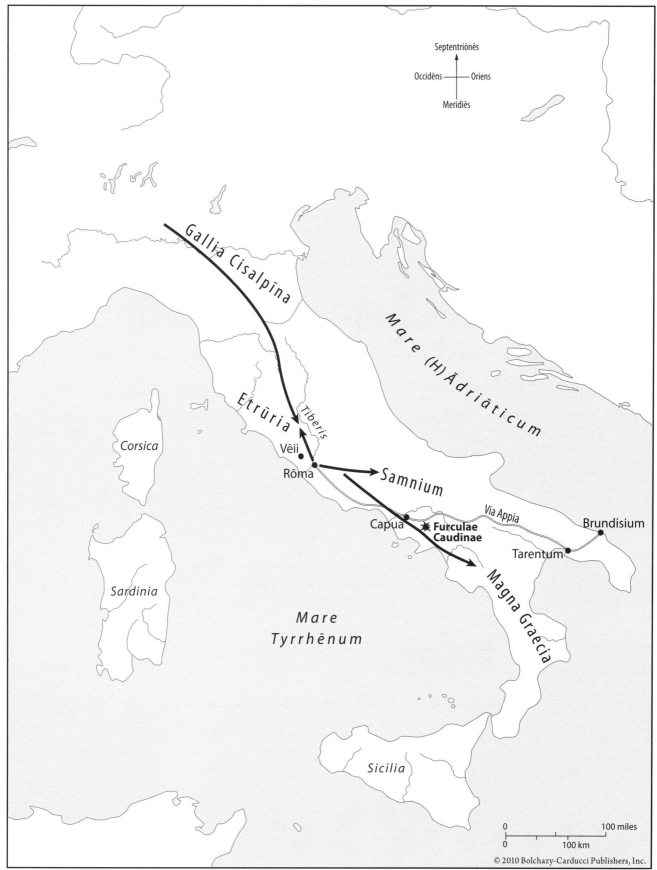

Septentriōnēs

Occidēns — Oriens

Merīdiēs

Gallia Cisalpīna

Mare (H)Ādriāticum

Etrūria

Tiberis

Corsica

Vēiī

Rōma

Samnium

Via Appia

Capua

★ **Furculae Caudīnae**

Brundisium

Tarentum

Magna Graecia

Sardinia

Mare Tyrrhēnum

Sicilia

0   100 miles

0   100 km

2. When was the Via Appia built? Why did Appius Claudius feel that a road was needed at this time?

_____

_____

_____

3. Research the ancient history of both Hēraclēa and Asculum. For what were they each known besides the war with Pyrrhus? Check Google Images to find archaeological evidence of Pyrrhus's use of elephants against Rome.

_____

_____

_____

TRANSLATION OF EXERCISE II

Respondē breviter Latīnē = Answer briefly in Latin.

1. Quī Vēiīs habitābant? = Who lived in Vēiī?

2. Cur Rōmānī tabulās historiae suae non habuērunt? = Why did the Romans not have records of their history?

3. Quis erat Pyrrhus? = Who was Pyrrhus?

Part II: The Punic Wars

If you locate the city of Carthāgō (Carthage) on the north coast of Africa, you will see that it is only about four hundred miles south of Rome and less than two hundred miles from the island of Sicily. Carthāgō was a wealthy port city founded in the ninth century BCE as a colony of Phoenicia. The Phoenicians were famous as seafarers and merchants. Phoenicia, their homeland, occupied the area that is now the country of Lebanon, but their trading routes took them all over the Mediterranean. One of the most famous trading products of the Phoenicians was a rare and very expensive dye made from a mollusk called a murex. The dye, known as Tyrian purple, takes its name from Tyrus (Tyre), one of the chief cities of Phoenicia.

As both cities grew in power and prosperity, Carthage and Rome became rivals. The Latin word for Phoenicians is Poenī, so the three wars between Carthage and Rome are called the Punic Wars. The focus of the initial conflict was Sicily. Both cities laid claim to the island, but since Carthage was primarily a sea power, and Rome's strength lay in her land forces, the First Punic War dragged on for more than twenty years, from 264 BCE to 241 BCE. The Romans eventually built their own navy, copying a Carthaginian warship they had captured, and won a decisive victory near the Aegātes (Aegadian Islands) off the coast of Sicily. This Roman victory brought an end to the First Punic War. After the war, Sicily became a Roman province, and Carthage was required to pay a large sum in settlement.

After the First Punic War, Carthage retained possession of her province of Spain, and there, in 219 BCE, the Carthaginian general Hannibal conducted a successful siege of Saguntum, a Spanish city allied with Rome. His victory over Saguntum gave him the supplies he needed for the enormous army of 100,000 soldiers and three dozen elephants he was assembling for an assault on Italy. After crossing the Hīberus (Ebro River), Hannibal led his forces across the Pȳrēnaeī Montēs (the Pyrénées), the Rhodanus (the Rhône River), and the Alpēs Montēs (the Alps). You can see his route on the map. He inflicted two crushing defeats on the forces of Rome, the first near the Trebia (Trebbia River) in December, 218 BCE and the second at Lacus Trasīmenus (Lake Trasimene) in June, 217 BCE. The following year, Hannibal again defeated a Roman army, this time at the battle of Cannae in Puglia. After Cannae, Hannibal and his army remained in Italy for more than ten years. He never actually attacked the city of Rome, but the Romans were unable to free themselves from the Carthaginians' presence until the Roman general Scipio invaded North Africa, and Hannibal was finally forced to withdraw from Italy. He was defeated at the battle of Zama in 202 BCE, and committed suicide in exile the following year.

Spain became a Roman province after the Second Punic War, and Rome again received a large settlement. However, the Third Punic War broke out in 149 BCE when Carthage began to rearm. The Roman army laid siege to Carthage, and at the end of three years, the Romans burned the city to the ground. They put the men of Carthage to death; the women and children were sold into slavery. North Africa became another province of Rome, and Carthage became one of the most prosperous and powerful cities in the Roman world.

EXERCISES

I. Highlight on the map:

1. Carthāgō (Carthage)
2. Sicilia (Sicily)
3. Aegātes (Aegadian Islands)
4. Hispānia (Spain)
5. Saguntum
6. Hīberus (Ebro River)

7. Rhodanus (Rhône River)
8. Trebia (Trebbia River)
9. Lacus Trasīmenus (Lake Trasimene)
10. Cannae
11. Zama

II. Label on the map:

1. Alpēs Montēs
2. Pȳrēnaeī Montēs

III. Give the Latin for the following.

1. Carthage   _____

2. Sicily   _____

3. Spain   _____

4. Rhône   _____

IV. Respondē breviter Latīnē.

1. Ubi est Carthāgō?

   _____

2. Quī Carthāginem aedificāvērunt?

   _____

3. Quis elephantōs mīlitēsque trans Alpēs dūxit?

   _____

ROMAN HISTORY: PUNIC WARS

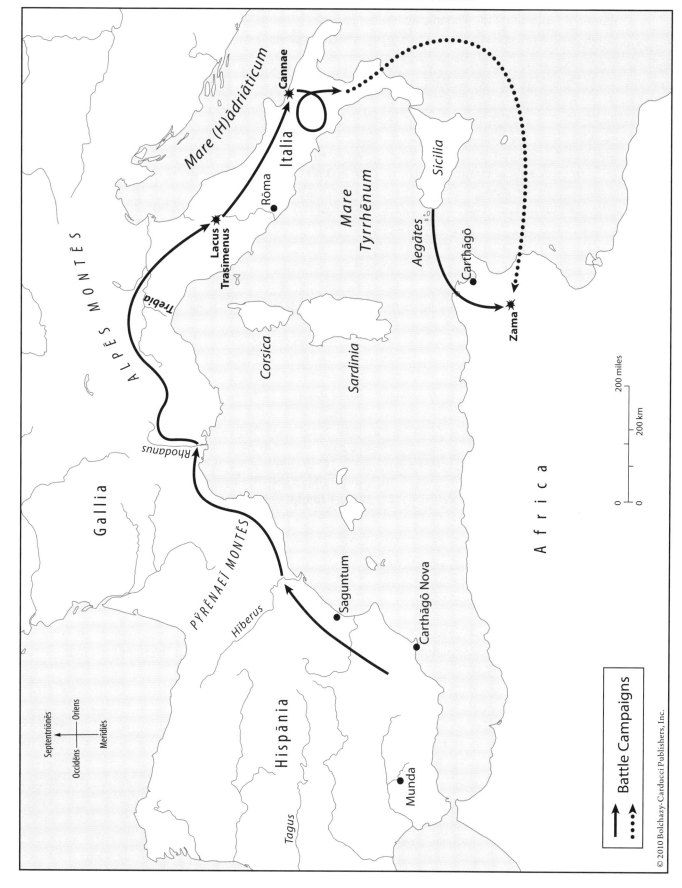

V.　Īre ulterius

1.　Find out more about the Phoenicians. What special characteristic of their alphabet sets it apart from other early writing systems such as Egyptian hieroglyphics?

_____

_____

_____

2.　Find out more about Hannibal's family. Who was his father? his brother?

_____

_____

_____

3.　What are the three parts of a Roman man's name called? What is an *agnōmen*? What *agnōmen* was Scipio given to honor his victories in the Punic Wars?

_____

_____

_____

4.　Who was Fabius Cunctātor? How did he oppose Hannibal's forces when they were occupying Italy? Explain the origin of his *agnōmen,* "Cunctātor." Find out about the political movement called Fabian socialism. Why was the movement named after Fabius Cunctātor?

_____

_____

_____

5.　After the Second Punic War what Roman official feared that Carthage would again threaten Rome? What was his famous saying about the destruction of Carthage? What does the saying mean in English?

_____

_____

_____

6. Read Book 4 of the *Aeneid*. How does Vergil explain the enmity between Rome and Carthage?

_____

_____

_____

_____

7. Who was the Roman hero Regulus? What was his mission? For what was he remembered?

_____

_____

_____

VI. Test yourself! Label the blank map with the following:

1. Hispānia (Spain)
2. Gallia (Gaul)
3. Rhodanus (Rhône River)
4. Italia (Italy)
5. Rōma (Rome)
6. Sicilia (Sicily)
7. Corsica
8. Sardinia
9. Pȳrēnaeī Montēs (Pyrénées)
10. Alpēs Montēs (Alps)
11. Trasimēnus Lacus (Lake Trasimene)
12. Cannae
13. Mare (H)Ādriāticum (Adriatic Sea)
14. Africa (North Africa)
15. Carthāgō (Carthage)
16. Zama

Translation of Exercise IV

Respondē breviter Latīnē = Answer briefly in Latin.

1. Ubi est Carthāgō? = Where is Carthage?

2. Quī Carthāginem aedificāvērunt? = Who built Carthage?

3. Quis elephantōs mīlitēsque trans Alpēs dūxit? = Who led elephants and soldiers across the Alps?

ROMAN HISTORY: PUNIC WARS

Part III: The Roman Empire

After Rome's conquest of Carthage in the Punic Wars, her armies waged new wars in other parts of the Mediterranean world. By the end of the second century BCE, Macedonia, Greece, and Asia had all become provinces of Rome. However, the following century was marked in Italy by almost continuous civil unrest and a devastating series of political rivalries. Finally, in 31 BCE, Octāvius, Iūlius Caesar's great nephew and heir, defeated the forces of Antony and Cleopatra in a sea battle at Actium off the west coast of Greece. With this victory, he became the sole leader of the Roman world. Octavius, who is also known as Augustus, took the title *princeps* (first citizen). His reign, from 31 BCE to 14 CE, is thus known as the Principate. Augustus's successors are called the Julio-Claudian emperors. They were the first dynasty to rule the Roman Empire.

If you look at the map, you can see the extent of Rome's dominions under Augustus. Notice that all of North Africa, including Egypt, was under Rome's control. Dalmatia, on the eastern coast of the Mare (H)Ādrāticum (Adriatic Sea), and Pannonia, just south of the Rhēnus (Rhine), had also become Roman provinces. Augustus himself attempted to conquer additional territory north of the Rhēnus, but his army suffered a humiliating defeat at the hands of the Germans in the Battle of Teutoburg Forest in 9 CE. Following this defeat, Augustus grew more cautious, and he warned his successors against over-expansion. In spite of Augustus' warning, Britannia and Maurētānia in North Africa became provinces while Claudius was emperor, and Iūdaea, once a client kingdom of Rome, came under direct Roman authority in 4 BCE. On the map find the Bosporus Kingdom, this client kingdom populated by Greeks, never became a Roman province.

The Roman Empire reached its largest extent under the Emperor Trajan in the early second century CE. Trajan himself won victories north of the Dānuvius (Danube) in eastern Europe in the region known as Dācia, and you can see from the map that Rome under Trajan controlled more than half of Europe, all of North Africa, and much of the Middle East. Toward the end of his rule, Trajan had begun to withdraw from the eastern provinces. Indeed, control over Armenia only lasted three years (114–117 CE), Assyria just two years (116–117 CE), and Mesopotamia but a year (116–117 CE). Trajan's immediate successor Hadrian began to draw in the boundaries of the empire. Hadrian set the Dānuvius (Danube) as the limit of Rome's dominions in eastern Europe, and as you know, he established a frontier in northern England by building Hadrian's Wall. After Hadrian's reign, the territory of the Roman Empire continued to shrink as later emperors faced civil unrest and dynastic quarrels. They also faced pressure on the borders of the empire from northern tribes. In 284 CE, the emperor Diocletian divided the empire into two administrative units with an "augustus" assisted by a "caesar" ruling in each. This arrangement was known as the tetrarchy (rule by four). Diocletian retired in 305 CE, and after a brief period of civil war, Constantine became the new emperor. Constantine reunited the empire, but he moved the capital from Rome to Bȳzantium, which he renamed Constantīnopolis. The empire was divided again in 395 CE. This time the division was final. The eastern empire with Constantīnopolis as its capital flourished until it was captured by the Ottoman Turks in 1453. The western empire with Rome as its capital suffered invasion after invasion. Most scholars agree that its end came in 476 when the Goth Odoacer overthrew the last emperor of Rome, Romulus Augustulus.

EXERCISES

I. Highlight on the map:

1. Britannia (Britain)
2. Dānuvius (Danube)
3. Rhēnus (Rhine)
4. Dācia
5. German tribes
6. Gallia (Gaul)
7. Hierosolyma (Jerusalem)
8. Arabia
9. Armenia
10. Dācia
11. Nōricum
12. Pontus
13. Aquītānia
14. Baetica
15. Cilicia
16. Germānia Inferior

II. Respondē breviter Latīnē.

1. Quid est nōmen alterum Octāvī?

    _____

2. Quis erat imperator Rōmānus quandō Britannia prōvincia facta est?

    _____

III. Īre ulterius

Find out more about one of the following emperors. Give dates of birth and death and two or three significant facts about each one's reign.

Augustus _____

_____

_____

Trajan _____

_____

_____

Hadrian _____

_____

_____

ROMAN HISTORY: ROMAN EMPIRE UNDER TRAJAN

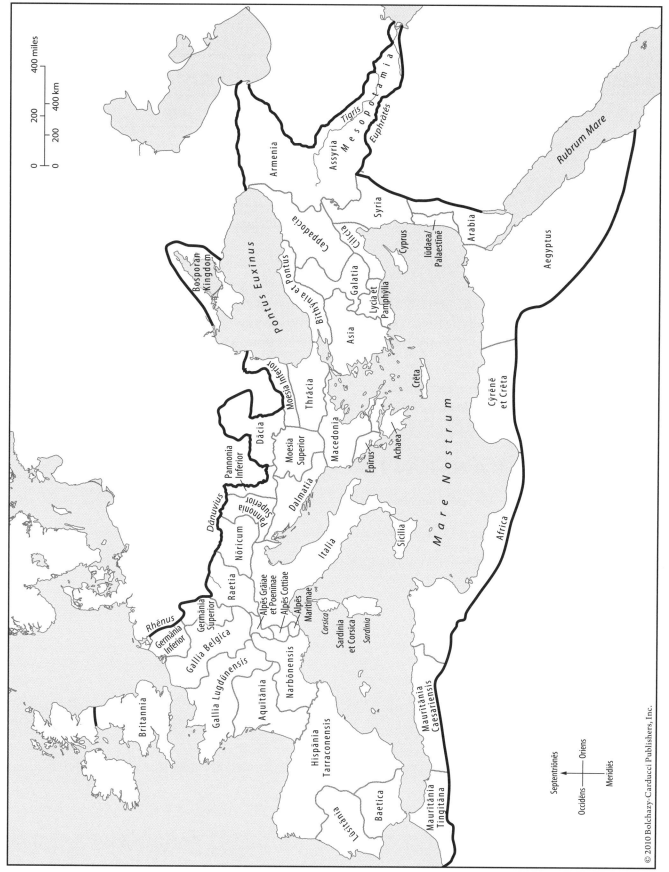

400 miles

200

400 km

200

0

0

Mesopotamia

Tigris

Euphrātēs

Rubrum Mare

Armenia

Assyria

Syria

Cappadocia

Cilicia

Cyprus

Iūdaea/
Palaestinē

Arabia

Aegyptus

Bosporān
Kingdom

Pontus Euxīnus

Bithȳnia et Pontus

Galatia

Asia

Lycia et
Pamphȳlia

Crēta

Cȳrēnē
et Crēta

Moesia Inferior

Thrācia

Macedonia

Mare Nostrum

Dācia

Moesia
Superior

Epīrus

Achaea

Pannonia
Inferior

Dānuvius

Dalmatia

Pannonia
Superior

Nōricum

Italia

Sicilia

Africa

Raetia

Alpēs Grāiae
et Poenīnae

Alpēs Cottiae

Alpēs
Maritimae

Corsica

Sardinia
et Corsica

Sardinia

Rhēnus

Germānia
Inferior

Germānia
Superior

Gallia Belgica

Narbōnensis

Gallia Lugdūnensis

Aquitānia

Mauritānia
Caesariensis

Britannia

Hispānia
Tarraconensis

Baetica

Lūsitānia

Mauritānia
Tingitāna

Septentriōnēs

Oriens

Occidēns

Meridiēs

© 2010 Bolchazy-Carducci Publishers, Inc.

Diocletian _____

_____

_____

Constantine _____

_____

_____

IV.   Roman History Projects

1.   Prepare a PowerPoint™ presentation about one of the following:

- The Punic Wars

- Roads and Aqueducts of the Roman Empire

2.   Research each of the provinces shown on the map. Find out when and how they become Roman provinces. Who was ruling Rome at the time they became provinces? Is that reflected in the province's name? What country(ies) today includes this Roman province? Discuss 2–3 significant facts about each province.

NB: For this assignment, each student can be assigned a province or provinces depending on class size and then each would give a mini-presentation to the class using PowerPoint™ or a similar format.

TRANSLATION OF EXERCISE II

Respondē breviter Latīnē = Answer briefly in Latin.

1.   Quid est nōmen alterum Octāvī? = What is another name of Octavius?

2.   Quis erat imperator Rōmānus quandō Britannia prōvincia facta est? = Who was the Roman emperor when Britain became a province?

VIII. Graecia

Greece

The Roman poet Horace once wrote "Captive Greece took captive her uncivilized conqueror" (*Epistulae* 2.156). What a perfect summing up of the deep and enduring cultural connection between Greece and Rome! Most upper class Romans spoke Greek as well as Latin, and after Greece became a Roman province in the second century BCE, it was customary for well-to-do young Romans to spend time in Athens studying philosophy and rhetoric as part of their education. One of Cicero's greatest friends, Titus Pompōnius, moved to Athens as a young man. He remained in Greece for most of his life and was known as Atticus because he loved Athens so much, and the area around Athens is called Attica.

As you know, Roman travelers bound for Greece set sail from Brundisium on the east coast of Italy. Opposite Brundisium across the Adriatic was the busy port of Durrachium. What would a young Roman like Atticus or Horace expect to find after he landed in Greece? Almost certainly he would have been aware of the harsh terrain of the Greek peninsula. The Greeks themselves promoted the view that Macedonia, the northern part of the Greek peninsula, was an especially forbidding and uncivilized region. A Roman would have known that Athēnae (Athens) lay near the east coast in the hilly central portion of the peninsula, and that Sparta was located in the Peloponnēsus, the rugged southern region of the peninsula. He might remember that the area around Sparta was known as Lacōnia. Would he have heard tales of the fabulous riches and decadence of Corinthus (Corinth), a city on the narrow strip of land that joins the Peloponnēsus to the rest of Greece? This bridge of land is known as the Isthmus of Corinth. The Emperor Nero had a plan to dig a canal through the isthmus, but, as you know, his plan was never realized, and ships going from the Adriatic to the Aegean were put on rollers and dragged across the isthmus.

A young Roman would have heard of the sanctuary of Olympia in the western Peloponnēsus because the Olympic Games were held there every four years beginning in 776 BCE, and he would surely have read about Mycēnae, home to the Homeric king Agamemnon. If he knew the myth of Oedipus, he would also have known that Thēbae (Thebes), the town of Oedipus's birth, was located not far from Athēnae. Would he perhaps have heard of another ancient city called Thebes? Would he have known that the other Thebes is not in Greece at all, but in Egypt?

For a young Roman with a knowledge of mythology, many of the mountains of Greece would have had a special appeal. For example, Cyllēne Mōns in the Peloponnēsus near Corinthus was celebrated as the birthplace of the god Mercury. Helicōn Mōns and Parnāsus Mōns, were both associated with Apollo and the Muses. People came from all over the ancient world to consult Apollo's oracle at Delphī just south of Parnāsus. Greek myth held that Delphī was the center of the world. In the northeast, Pēlion Mōns was home to the kindly centaur Chiron, tutor of Achilles. Olympus Mōns itself, home of the gods of Greek mythology, lies to the north of Pēlion Mōns, its lofty peak shrouded in clouds.

The islands that line the western coast of Greece would also have had interesting associations for an ancient traveler. As he caught sight of the island of Ithaca, he might have remembered Homer's *Odyssey* and been amazed at the great distance Odysseus and his men had to travel to arrive home after the Trojan War. And he would have been aware of the historical importance of Corcȳra (Corfu), another large island off the west coast of Greece, because he would have known that Corcȳra's quarrel with the city of Corinth was one of the causes of the Peloponnesian War.

South of the Peloponnēsus, the largest and most famous of the Greek islands was Crēta (Crete), once the center of the rich and vibrant Minoan civilization. The name Minoan comes from Mīnōs, a son of Zeus and legendary king of Crete. Any educated Roman would have been familiar with the myth of the Mīnōtaurus (Minotaur), a terrible man-eating monster, half man and half bull. According to legend, King Minos imprisoned the Minotaur in a labyrinth within his palace, but his daughter Ariadnē helped the Athenian prince Thēsēus enter the labyrinth, kill the Minotaur, and escape from Crete. Thēsēus later abandoned the sleeping Ariadnē on the island of Naxos in his haste to return to Athens.

Thēra (Santorini), another island north of Crete, is also related to the Cretan saga: Thēra's curious half moon outline is the result of a powerful volcanic eruption that occurred ca. 1400 BCE. The eruption not only changed the shape of Thēra, but also destroyed a number of small islands nearby and ended the Minoan civilization on the island of Crēta.

The islands north of Thēra are called the Cycladēs. One of the most famous of the Cycladēs is Dēlos. Certainly a young Roman would know Dēlos as the birthplace of the god Apollo, and he would be aware of the tradition forbidding anyone from dying or being born on the island of Dēlos. If our ancient voyager had read Vergil's *Aeneid*, or was a native of Campānia, he would also remember that the settlers of Cūmae on the Bay of Naples came originally from Euboea, the large island off the coast of Attica.

Of course, any student of Roman history would undoubtedly recall that the battles of Pharsālus and Philippī were fought on Greek soil. Pharsālus lies in central Greece, southwest of Mt. Pelion. Here, in 48 BCE, Julius Caesar defeated the forces of his former ally and fellow triumvir Pompey. After Caesar's death in 44 BCE, the troops of Mark Antony and Caesar's heir Octāvius, later known as Augustus, defeated the army of Caesar's assassins at the Battle of Philippī. Horace himself fought at Philippī although he reported that he ran away in the midst of the battle. If you have read Shakespeare's *Julius Caesar*, you may remember that the last act takes place the night before the battle. Philippī lies on the edge of the region of Thrace. In 31 BCE, Octāvius, with the assistance of his right hand man Agrippa, defeated the forces of Mark Antony and Cleopatra in a sea battle fought off the western coast of Greece at Actium.

A young man who had read Herodotus's *Persian Wars* might also have been interested in other battles fought long ago in Greece. For example, during the first campaign of the Persian Wars in 490 BCE, the Athenian army defeated a much larger Persian army on the plain of Marathōn, which is in Attica 26 miles northeast of Athens. After the victory, an Athenian runner named Phidippides is said to have run from Marathon to Athens. Phidippides had just returned from a mission to Sparta seeking reinforcements to thwart the Persian invasion so he was probably already weary. Nevertheless, according to legend, he dashed to Athens, cried out "We have won!" and then died. The 26-mile distance of a modern marathon is based on Phidippides's famous run.

In a second phase of the Persian Wars in 480 BCE, the Persian king Xerxes led a vast Persian army south toward Athens. A small band of Spartans intercepted the Persian force at Thermopylae, a mountain pass on the Gulf of Mālia that separates Euboea from the mainland. The Spartans, hugely outnumbered, were all killed, but their gallant fight delayed the Persians and allowed the Athenians to evacuate the city and to assemble a fleet of small ships. These maneuverable Athenian ships were able to defeat the Persian fleet at the battle of Salamis. The battle takes its name from the island of Salamis, which lies southwest of Piraeus in the Saronic Gulf.

Let us now leave our fictional traveler and turn our attention to the coast of Asia Minor and the islands that line the shore. This entire region was colonized by settlers from the mainland of Greece and for centuries played an important role both in Greek history and in Greek literature. Let us begin with the area to the east of the Greek mainland. First, locate the Pontus Euxīnus (Black Sea) and remember that the district south of the sea is called Bīthȳnia. The capital of Bīthȳnia was Amastris. Another important city in Bīthȳnia was Nīcaea, famous as the meeting place of Christian clerics convened by the emperor Constantine in 325 CE. The Council of Nīcaea established the Nicene Creed, which describes the Christian god as a trinity.

Southwest of Bīthȳnia lies an area called Phrygia. You may have encountered the phrase phrygian cap in a history class. This distinctive turban was associated with the *pīleus* or cap of freedom worn by former slaves in Rome and adopted as a symbol of freedom centuries later in revolutionary France. It even appears on the seal of the US Senate.

Now, locate the city of Bȳzantium, later called Constantīnopolis and known today as Istanbul. As you remember from an earlier chapter, Istanbul is commonly understood as a corruption of the Greek phrase εις την πολιν, "into/to the city." Followers of Greek Orthodoxy, however, continue to refer to the city as Constantīnopolis, headquarters for their church and patriarch, the head of their church. Notice the strategic location of Bȳzantium on the Bosphorus, the narrow strait leading from the Pontus Euxīnus into a smaller body of water called the Propontis or Sea of Marmora. The name Propontis is appropriate when you know that the Latin word *prō* can mean "in front of, before." Marmora also makes sense because the Latin word for marble is *marmor* and several islands in the sea were known for their marble quarries.

At the mouth of the Sea of Marmora where it flows into the Mare Aegaeum (the Aegean Sea), you can see a narrow channel. This is the Hellespontus (Hellespont). Here, according to mythology, the doomed lover Leander drowned as he tried to swim across to meet his beloved Hero who lived on the opposite shore. Here, the Greek historian Herodotus tells us, the Persian king Xerxes built two bridges of boats in order to move his troops into Greece for the campaign against the Greek cities of Athens and Sparta in 480 BCE. His cavalry crossed on one bridge, his infantry on the other, and the whole army was so large that it took seven days and nights for it to cross the Hellespontus.

You can see that the legendary city of Trōia/Īlium (Troy) was located on the Aegean coast at the southern end of the Hellespontus. Because of its location, Troy had access to all the ships sailing in and out of the Black Sea. No wonder the city was renowned for its wealth! The peninsula on which Troy stood is called the Troad, and the river of Troy is the Scamander. Īda Mōns (Mt. Ida) lies southeast of the city. It is interesting that there is a second Īda Mōns on the island of Crete. The Cretan mountain is associated with the birth of Zeus.

Note the rich coastal city of Ephesus, famous as the center for worship of the goddess Diana. The massive temple to Diana/Artemis at Ephesus was one of the seven wonders of the ancient world, and you may know that the apostle Paul was driven from Ephesus because the silversmiths were afraid their trade in votive offerings for Diana's temple would dry up.

Just as Diana was worshipped at Ephesus, so the goddess Venus was venerated on the island of Cyprus off the coast of ancient Syria. Idalium, Amalthus, and Golgi were all towns on Cyprus known for their shrines to Venus. Other islands along the coast of Asia Minor south of Troy include Lesbos, home of the Greek poet Sappho, as well as Chios, Icaria, Samos, Cnidos, and Rhodus. Cnidos is famous for a beautiful statue of Venus called the Venus of Cnidos found on the island while Rhodus was known for the colossal statue that guarded its harbor.

Exercises

I.   Highlight on the map of Greece:

1.   Athēnae (Athens)
2.   Sparta
3.   Attica
4.   Euboea
5.   Peloponnēsus (Peloponnese)
6.   Olympia
7.   Corinthus (Corinth)
8.   Delphī
9.   Dēlos
10. Thēra (Santorini)
11. Crēta (Crete)
12. Ithaca
13. Corcȳra (Corfu)
14. Marathōn

15. Thermopylae
16. Aegaeum Mare (Aegean Sea)
17. Īonium Mare (Ionian Sea)
18. Pontus Euxīnus (the Black Sea)
19. Bīthȳnia
20. Bȳzantium (Constantīnopolis/Istanbul)
21. Propontis (Sea of Marmora)
22. Hellespontus (Hellespont)
23. Trōia/Īlium (Troy)
24. Lesbos
25. Samos
26. Cnidos
27. Rhodus (Rhodes)
28. Ephesus

II.   List the following.

1.   five (5) famous Greek mountains:

_____

2.   five (5) famous Greek islands:

_____

3.   five (5) famous battle sites in Greece:

_____

4.   five (5) famous cities in Asia Minor or in Greece:

_____

III. Name the following.

1.   the strait that Xerxes bridged in 480 BCE: _____

2.   the island where Apollo was born: _____

Ancient Greece

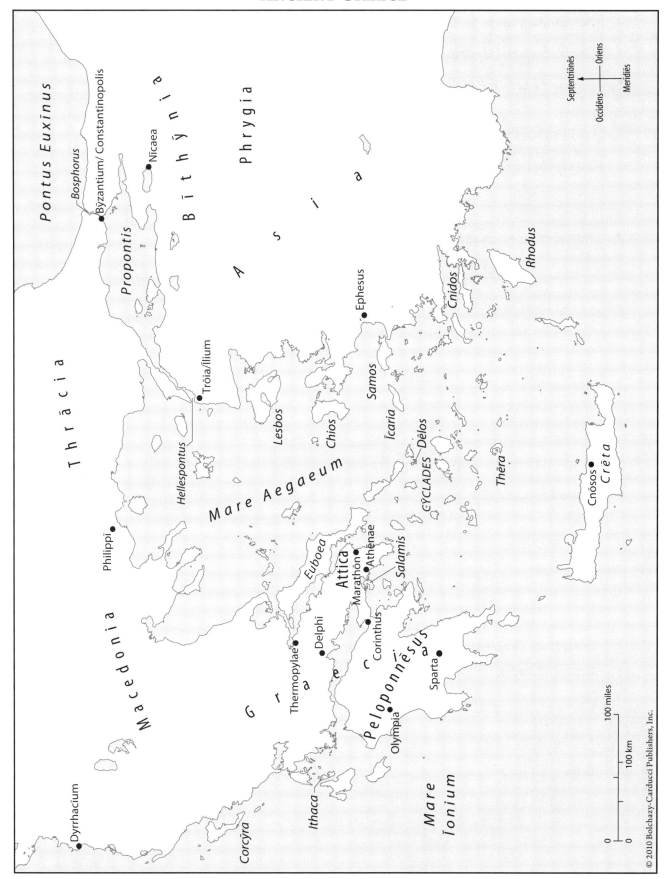

3. the site of Apollo's oracle: _____

4. the mountain where Mercury was born: _____

5. the island where Odysseus lived: _____

6. the island where Thēsēus left Ariadnē: _____

IV. Respondē breviter Latīnē.

1. Quid est portus Athēnārum?

   _____

2. Ubi habitābat Mīnōtaurus?

   _____

3. Quis Mīnōtaurum interfēcit?

   _____

4. In quā īnsulā Ariadnē relicta est?

   _____

V. Test yourself! Label the blank map with the following:

1. Pontus Euxīnus

2. Bīthȳnia

3. Bȳzantium (Istanbul)

4. Bosphorus

5. Propontis (Sea of Marmora)

6. Hellespontus

7. Trōia/Īlium (Troy)

8. Rhodus (Rhodes)

9. Dēlos

10. Thēra (Santorini)

11. Crēta (Crete)

12. Ithaca

13. Athēnae (Athens)

14. Attica

15. Sparta

16. Peloponnēsus (Peloponnese)

17. Olympia

18. Corinthus (Corinth)

19. Delphī

20. Marathōn

21. Thermopylae

22. Aegaeum (Aegean)

23. Iōnium (Ionian)

24. Euboea

ANCIENT GREECE

VI. Īre ulterius

1. Find information about the myth of Helle and the golden ram. Retell the myth.

_____

_____

_____

2. Find information about the myth that explains how the Aegean Sea acquired its name. Retell the myth. Be sure to explain who Aegeus was and why he kept watching the sea.

_____

_____

_____

3. Do research on the island of Dēlos. Retell the myth of the birth of Apollo and Diana. Describe the archaeological remains found on the island. Find information on the Delian League. When was it established? Why was its treasury on the island of Dēlos?

_____

_____

_____

4. Do research on Apollo's oracle at Delphī. What was his priestess called? What are some famous examples of advice given by the oracle?

_____

_____

_____

5. You know that the area around Sparta was called Lacōnia. What does the English word "laconic" mean?

_____

6. Find out more about the phrygian cap or *pīleus*. Find examples of works of art that use the *pīleus* as a symbol of liberty. You might consult the website of the US Senate.

_____

_____

_____

7. What does the phrase "to pile Pēlion on Ossa" mean? Retell the myth from which the phrase comes.

_____

_____

_____

8. What important event in the history of the early Christian church took place in Philippī?

_____

_____

_____

9. What is the epitaph of the Spartans who died at the Battle of Themopylae?

_____

_____

_____

VII. Projects for Greece

1. Write a skit based on one of the myths mentioned in this chapter.

2. Create an enlarged map of Greece with all the place names written in Greek letters.

3. Find out about the lives of the Macedonian kings, Philip and Alexander the Great. Prepare a map showing the campaigns of each. NB: Alexander's victories took him as far as India so make sure that your map is large enough to show all of his expeditions.

4. Pick one of the archeological sites listed below. Find and print pictures from Google Images. Arrange the pictures on a poster for your classroom. Be sure that you can point out the location of your site on a map of Greece!
   - Verginia
   - Dēlos
   - Delphī
   - Olympia
   - Cnōsus

5. If you are a student of the poet Catullus, refer to Carmen 4 and Carmen 36, and prepare a map with each of the places named by Catullus.

6. Visit http://edsitement.neh.gov/lesson-plan/alphabet-historic-greek-alphabet-more-familiar-you-think. Learn about the development of the Greek alphabet. Share what you have learned with your class.

7. Read the account of the battle of Thermopylae in Herodotus's *Persian Wars*. Then watch the movie *300*. Report to your class the ways in which the movie is true to Herodotus and the ways in which it differs.

8. Find out more about Cicero's friend Atticus. Write in English an imaginary exchange of letters between the two men about the purchase by Atticus of certain statues for Cicero's country villa, or about Atticus's planned publication of one of Cicero's orations.

ANCIENT GREECE CERTAMEN

1. What is the modern name for the Pontus Euxīnus?

   Bonus 1: Where are the cities of Nīcaea and Amastris?

   Bonus 2: Who convened a meeting of clerics in Nīcaea in 325 CE?

2. Where is Phrygia?

   Bonus 1: What is another name for the turban called a Phrygian cap?

   Bonus 2: What does the *pīleus* or Phrygian cap symbolize?

3. What important city is located on the strait called the Bosphorus?

   Bonus 1: From what sea does the Bosphorus flow?

   Bonus 2: What is another name for the Propontis?

4. What did Leander have to swim across in order to visit his beloved Hero?

   Bonus 1: What Persian king built two bridges across the Hellespont?

   Bonus 2: Into what sea does the Hellespont flow?

5. Complete this analogy: Tiberis : Rōma :: Scamander : _____

   Bonus 1: What is another name for Troy?

   Bonus 2: Name a famous mountain near Troy that has the same name as the mountain in Crete associated with the birth of Zeus.

6. What goddess was worshipped in Ephesus?

   Bonus 1: What poet is associated with the island of Lesbos?

   Bonus 2: What island is associated with the legend of Theseus?

7.   What is the modern name for the island of Thēra?

    Bonus 1: What destroyed Cretan civilization?

    Bonus 2: Who was the mythological king of Crete?

8.   With what god is the island of Dēlos associated?

    Bonus 1: What is the name of the large group of islands to which Dēlos belongs?

    Bonus 2: Where is the shrine to Apollo on the mainland of Greece?

9.   What was the ancient name for the island of Corfu?

    Bonus 1: The Peloponnesian War began with a quarrel between Corcyra and what city?

    Bonus 2: What was the name of the island that was home to Odysseus?

10.   Mt. Cyllēne : Mercury :: Mt. Parnassus : _____

    Bonus 1: What mountain was home to Chirōn, the centaur?

    Bonus 2: What does it mean "to pile Pēlion on Ossa"?

11.   What is the port of Athens called?

    Bonus 1: What is the area around Athens called?

    Bonus 2: What is the island northeast of Attica called?

12.   Where did the Greeks from Euboea settle?

    Bonus 1: What is the name for the southern part of the Greek peninsula?

    Bonus 2: What is the name of the area around Sparta?

13.   What event was held every four years beginning in 776 BCE?

    Bonus 1: What city was home to the Homeric king Agamemnon?

    Bonus 2: Name the city on the narrow isthmus between the Peloponnēsus and the rest of the mainland of Greece.

14.   In what city was Oedipus born?

    Bonus 1: Where is another city called Thebes?

    Bonus 2: What happened at Thermopylae?

15. Why did Phidippides run from Marathon to Athens?

   Bonus 1: How far did he run?

   Bonus 2: What happened when he arrived in Athens?

TRANSLATION OF EXERCISE IV

Respondē breviter Latīnē = Answer briefly in Latin.

1. Quid est portus Athēnārum? = What is the port of Athens?

2. Ubi habitābat Mīnōtaurus? = Where did the Minotaur live?

3. Quis Mīnōtaurum interfēcit? = Who killed the Minotaur?

4. In quā īnsulā Ariadnē relicta est? = On what island was Ariadne abandoned?

IX. Athēnae
Athens

If you visit Athēnae (Athens) today, you will see that the modern city has risen amid the ruins of a fabled past. Interestingly, you will find that a number of monuments like the Tower of the Winds owe their existence to Romans such as the emperor Hadrian. You may also recognize some landmarks like the Arēopagus if you are familiar with the New Testament account of the journeys of the Apostle Paul.

At the heart of the city stands the Ācropolis. *Acro* in Greek means high, and *polis* means city, and indeed the rugged rock-strewn hill dominates the skyline of the ancient city. Its steep slopes provided protection to the earliest inhabitants of the city. Later, it became the site of some of Athens' most important shrines. In the fifth century BCE a grand entrance called the Propylaea was constructed on the west side of the hill. Just south of the Propylaea, you can see the small temple of Athēna Nike. *Nike* means "victory" in Greek, and the present temple was built during the Peloponnesian War when Athens was locked in conflict with Sparta but still hoped for a resounding victory.

Of course, the Parthenon, a larger and much more famous shrine to Athena, crowns the Ācropolis. It is one of the best-known buildings in the world. It takes its name from Athena's epithet *Parthenia*, which means maiden. The Parthenon was built during the rule of the Athenian statesman Pericles in the fifth century BCE after the Athenian victory over the Persians. This temple was built over the foundations of the earlier temple that the Persians had burned. Pericles envisioned the new, magnificent Parthenon as a symbol of Athens' triumph over the Persians, of the triumph of Athenian democracy. Inside the temple stood the sculptor Phidias's magnificent statue of Athena. The Parthenon today is without a roof because it was used for arms storage in the seventeenth century, and it was damaged by an explosion of gunpowder. In the early nineteenth century, much of the decorative sculpture from the Parthenon was taken to England by a British nobleman named Lord Elgin. Today the so called Elgin Marbles are housed in the British Museum in London. In 2009, the Greek government opened a new museum to house various artifacts and objets d'art from the acropolis. The museum includes space to display the Elgin Marbles, which the Greeks have asked be returned.

Near the Parthenon on the Ācropolis stands an even more ancient temple called the Erechthēum. It takes its name from a legendary early king of Athens called Erectheus. The building is famous for its columns in the form of maidens. These are called the Caryatids, and five of the originals have been removed to the new museum to save them from the corrosive effects of air pollution. In addition, one is in the British Museum.

One of the oldest and best preserved temples in Greece, known as the Hēphaistion or the Thēseīon, is not on the Ācropolis at all. You can locate it at the northwest end of an open area called the Agorā. Originally a residential area, the Agorā became an outdoor meeting place similar to the Forum in Rome. Interestingly, it is here in the Agorā that archeologists have found large numbers of *ostraka*, bits of pottery on which the citizens inscribed the names of leaders they wanted exiled.

Overlooking the Agorā to the southwest you will see the Arēopagus, a hill remembered as the site of a famous court. Its name is related to Ares, the Greek god of war, the counterpart of the Roman Mars. The New Testament book of Acts has an account of the Apostle Paul's visit to Athens and the sermon he preached on the Arēopagus. Paul's sermon appealed to the logic of the Athenians. He noted that with Christianity's monotheism, one need not worry about a shrine to "the unknown god" as the Athenians had erected on the Arēopagus. Southwest of the Arēopagus you can see a semicircular structure labeled the Pnyx. Here, adult male citizens of Athens gathered to vote. Women, as you might deduce, were not enfranchised.

At the foot of the Ācropolis to the south you can see two theaters: the Ōdēum of Hērōdes Atticus and the Theater of Dionȳsus. The Ōdēum was built in the first century CE as a Roman style theater while the Greek style Theater of Dionȳsus dates from the fourth century BCE. If you have read the works of the great Greek playwrights Aeschylus, Sophocles, Euripides, and Aristophanes, you know that their works were performed here at a spring festival in honor of Dionȳsus, the god of wine and drama.

Not far from the Theater of Dionȳsus, southeast of the Ācropolis, you can see an enormous rectangular structure labeled the Temple of Olympian Zeus. By the time the Roman Emperor Hadrian completed this edifice in the second century CE, it had been under construction for several centuries. It measures 134 by 108 feet with huge columns 55.5 feet high and 6.5 feet in diameter. Much of the stone was used for other buildings in the Middle Ages, but the remaining columns still tower over the surrounding area.

Before you turn from the city plan of Athens, you should note the city walls. To the east the Emperor Hadrian extended the city, and his extension lies outside the original fortifications. To the west, you can see an area just outside the city walls labeled the Outer Ceramīcus. This was the burial ground of the ancient city. Finally, you should notice the Long Walls that connected Athens to her port of Pīraeus. The first Long Walls were destroyed by the Persians in 480 BCE, but they were rebuilt in the fifth century BCE. The Long Walls meant that the city could be supplied by sea even during a siege.

EXERCISES

I. Highlight the following on the city plan:

1. Ācropolis
2. Propylaea
3. Temple of Athēna Nike
4. Parthenon
5. Erechthēum
6. Hēphaistion/Thēseīon
7. Agorā
8. Arēopagus
9. Pnyx
10. Ōdēum of Hērōdes Atticus
11. Theater of Dionȳsus
12. Temple of Olympian Zeus
13. Ceramīcus
14. Long Walls
15. Pīraeus

CITY OF ATHENS

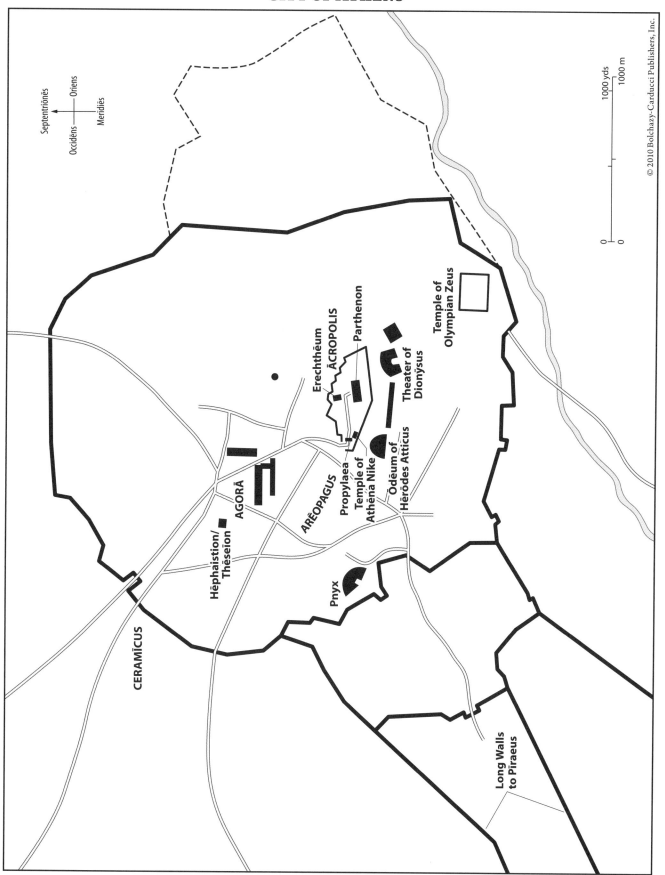

Septentriōnēs

Occidēns ——— Oriens

Merīdiēs

1000 yds
1000 m

0
0

Temple of
Olympian Zeus

Erechthēum
ACROPOLIS
Parthenon

Theater of
Dionȳsus

Propylaea
Temple of
Athēna Nike

Odēum of
Hērōdes Atticus

AREOPAGUS

Hēphaistion/
Thēseîon

AGORĀ

Pnyx

CERAMĪCUS

Long Walls
to Pīraeus

II. List the following.

　1. five (5) temples in Athens:

　　_____

　　_____

　2. two (2) meeting places of Athenian citizens:

　　_____

　3. two (2) places of entertainment in Athens:

　　_____

III. Translate these Greek words.

　1. acro　　　　　_____

　2. polis　　　　　_____

　3. parthenia　　　_____

　4. nike　　　　　_____

IV. Respondē breviter Latīnē.

　1. Quid est portus Athēnārum?

　　_____

　2. Quid est templum antīquissimum in Agorā?

　　_____

　3. Quid est templum maximum Athēnīs?

　　_____

　4. Dīc Latīnē *parthenia*:

　　_____

V.   Īre ulterius

1.   What English word comes from the Greek word *ostrakon*? What does it mean?

_____

_____

2.   Retell the myth of Orestes and the Furies.

_____

_____

_____

3.   Retell the myth of the death of King Aegeus, the father of Theseus.

_____

_____

_____

4.   Think about the word *ācropolis*. Find three English words that begin with *ācro*. Define each.

_____

_____

_____

5.   Investigate the building type called a stoa. What was its purpose? How many were in the area of the Agorā? What did you learn about the Stoa of Attalus? How did Stoic philosophy acquire its name?

_____

_____

_____

VI.   Projects for Athens

1.   Use pieces of a broken terra cotta flower pot and make ostraka. Write the name of an ancient Greek leader on each shard. Use Greek letters.

2.   Use poster board and make replicas of the masks worn by actors in the Theater of Dionysus. You should make one for comedy, one for tragedy.

3. Posters

   Pick one of the following subjects. Find and print pictures from Google Images or make your own sketches. Arrange the pictures on a poster.

   - the Parthenon
   - the Erechthēum
   - the Thēseīon
   - the Temple of Olympian Zeus
   - the Theater of Dionȳsus
   - the Tower of the Winds

4. Explore the new museum of the Acropolis via the Internet and prepare a report for your classmates on its features.

TRANSLATION OF EXERCISE IV

Respondē breviter Latīnē = Answer briefly in Latin.

1. Quid est portus Athēnārum? = What is the port of Athens?

2. Quid est templum antīquissimum in Agorā? = What is the most ancient temple in the Agora?

3. Quid est templum maximum Athēnīs? = What is the biggest temple in Athens?

4. Dīc Latīnē *parthenia*: = Say *parthenia* in Latin.

X. Gallia
Gaul

In 58 BCE Gaius Iūlius Caesar became governor of Gaul. Over the next seven years he conducted a series of campaigns that he recorded in detail in his *Commentāriī dē bellō Gallicō*. Generations of Latin students have translated the concise prose of the *Commentāriī*. Each book of the *Commentāriī* covers one year of Caesar's governorship. Book 1, for example, opens with a discussion of the geography of Gaul followed by an account of Caesar's first two campaigns, one against the Helvētiī (Swiss), the other against the Germānī. Later books deal with Caesar's further operations in Germānia, his two expeditions to Britannia, and his attacks on the Belgae and the naval forces of the Venetī. In Book 6, Caesar describes some unusual animals he has heard about and some of the social and religious customs of the Gauls. The last book of the *Commentaries* focuses on the siege of Alesia and ends with the surrender of the great Gallic leader Vercingetorix.

A knowledge of the geography of ancient Gaul and Britain is essential to an understanding of Caesar's achievements. When you look at the map, you will notice immediately that the familiar boundaries of European countries like France, Belgium, the Netherlands, Germany and Italy do not exist. These boundaries are of modern origin. Gallia may be translated "France," but it is not synonymous with the country of today. Notice that what is currently a part of northern Italy is labeled Gallia Cisalpīna on the map. Caesar refers to this area as Gallia Citerior. *Cis* in Latin means "near," *citerior* means "nearer," and this part of Italy is indeed nearer to Rome than the part of Gaul beyond the Alps. On your map, locate the area labeled Prōvincia. It is also known as Gallia Ulterior (Further Gaul) or Gallia Transalpīna (Gaul across the Alps). You probably know that the Latin word *prōvincia* means province or district, and this region of southern France was the earliest of the provinces that later made up the Roman Empire. Prōvincia was controlled by the Romans before Caesar became governor of Gaul. Obviously, Caesar did not have to conquer this area; instead, he sought to protect it when the path of the Helvetian migration involved a route through Prōvincia.

In the famous opening lines of chapter one of Book 1 of the *Commentāriī*, Caesar explains that Gaul is divided into three parts. If your parents or grandparents took Latin, they may well remember this passage! You can clearly see the three divisions on the map. Caesar says that the Belgae occupy the area where today we find the low countries of Luxembourg, Belgium, and the Netherlands. He calls the southeastern region of France between the Pȳrēnaeī Montēs (Pyrénées mountains) and the Garumnus (Garonne River) the territory of the Aquītanī. The large central area is labeled Gallia Celtica because, according to Caesar, the native inhabitants, whom the Romans call Gallī, refer to themselves as Celtī. Notice the town of Alesia, a Celtic stronghold that Caesar took by siege in 52 BCE. Notice also that within Gallia Celtica individual tribes are indicated. These include the Venetī on the peninsula of Brittany in the northeast, as well as the Aeduī and the Sēquanī near Alesia.

In addition to the major divisions of Gaul, you should locate the Helvētiī (Swiss) on your map. This tribe inhabited the mountainous area that today is Switzerland. Their chief town was Genava on Lacus Lemanus, which we call Lake Geneva. From Lacus Lemanus the river Rhodanus (Rhône) flows into the Mediterranean at Massilia (Marseilles). Other important rivers to locate include the Arar (Saône), which is a tributary of the Rhodanus, and the Rhēnus (Rhine), which separated Germānia, from Gallia Celtica. Caesar bridged the Rhine in 55 BCE, and Book 4 of the *Commentāriī* includes a detailed description of the bridge Caesar constructed. In building the bridge, Caesar probably intended to demonstrate the technological superiority of the Romans and thereby scare the Germānī off. Consider the parallels with the modern strategy of "shock and awe." Notice that the river Sēquana (Seine) gave its name to the Sēquanī, a tribe that lived nearby. The city of Lutetia (Paris) is on the banks of the Sēquana in the territory of a tribe called the Parīsiī. Lutetia is thus sometimes called Lutetia Parīsiōrum, and this explains the origin of the name Paris. Southwest of Lutetia the Sēquana joins with the Mātrona, today called the Marne.

Before you leave the map of Gaul, be sure to locate Hispānia (Spain), the Alpēs Montēs (Alps), the Rubicō (Rubicon), the Tiberis, and, of course, Rōma (Rome).

EXERCISES

I.   Color each division of Gaul a different color. Then, highlight the following:

1. Gallia Cisalpīna/Gallia Citerior (Northern Italy)

2. Gallia Transalpīna/Gallia Ulterior/ Prōvincia (Southern France)

3. Belgae (Belgium and the Netherlands, i.e., the low countries)

4. Aquītanī

5. Gallia Celtica (central France)

6. Alesia

7. Lutetia (Paris)

8. Massilia (Marseilles)

9. Rōma (Rome)

10. Venetī (Brittany)

11. Aeduī

12. Sēquanī

13. Helvētiī (Swiss)

14. Nerviī

15. Arar (Saône)

16. Rhēnus (Rhine)

17. Dānuvius (Danube)

18. Sēquana (Seine)

19. Rhodanus (Rhône)

20. Mātrona (Marne)

21. Garumna (Garonne)

22. Tiberis (Tiber)

23. Rubicō (Rubicon)

24. Britannia (Britain)

25. Hispānia (Spain)

26. Germānia (Germany)

27. Pȳrēnaeī Montēs (Pyrénées)

28. Alpēs Montēs (Alps)

29. Lacus Lemanus (Lake Geneva)

30. Mare (H)Ādriāticum (Adriatic Sea)

Gaul

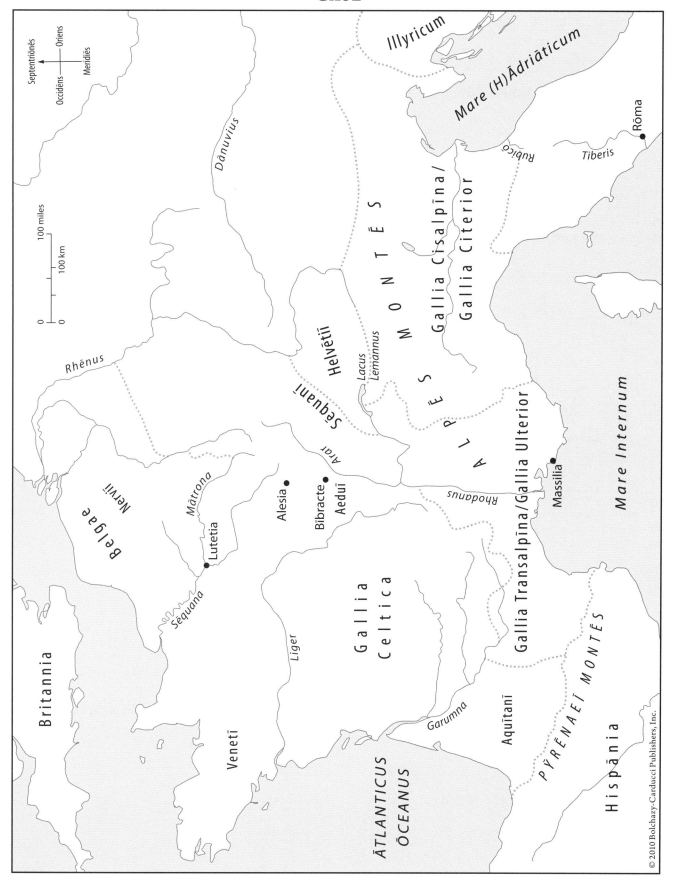

Septentriōnēs
Occidēns — Oriens
Merīdiēs

100 miles
100 km

Illyricum

Mare (H)Ādriāticum

Rōma

Rubicō

Tiberis

Dānuvius

MONTĒS

Gallia Cīsalpīna /
Gallia Citerior

Rhēnus

Helvētiī

Lacus
Lemannus

A L P Ē S

Sēquanī

Rhodanus

Mare Internum

Matrona

Arar

Gallia Transalpīna/Gallia Ulterior

Massilia

Belgae
Nerviī

Alesia

Bibracte
Aeduī

Lutetia

Sēquana

Gallia
Celtica

Liger

PYRĒNAEĪ MONTĒS

Britannia

Venetī

Garumna

Aquītānī

Hispānia

ĀTLANTICUS
ŌCEANUS

© 2010 Bolchazy-Carducci Publishers, Inc.

II. Respondē breviter Latīnē.

1. Quis erat Vercingetorix?

   _____

2. Quot partēs habēbat Gallia?

   _____

3. Ubi Caesar pōntem magnum aedificāvit?

   _____

4. Ubi sunt Alpēs Montēs?

   _____

III. Match:

1. _____ Helvētia   A. Lake Geneva
2. _____ Lutetia   B. Paris
3. _____ Garumna   C. Switzerland
4. _____ Mātrona   D. Marne River
5. _____ Sēquana   E. Seine River
6. _____ Rhodanus   F. Rhône River
7. _____ Rhēnus   G. Garonne River
8. _____ Gallia Cisalpīna H. Rhine River
9. _____ Hispānia   I. Southern France
10. _____ Lacus Lemanus   J. Saône River
11. _____ Gallia Transalpīna (Prōvincia) K. Northern Italy
12. _____ Arar   L. Spain

IV. Īre ulterius

1. Find out the name for the southern region of modern France around Marseilles. Explain its derivation.

   _____

2. What is Lake Geneva called in French?

   _____

3. What was the title of the queen of England who was the wife of Henry II and mother of Richard the Lion Hearted? Of what part of France was she a native?

_____

4. Read (or translate) and summarize these famous passages of *Caesar's Gallic Wars*.

Chapter 1 of Book 1: the divisions of Gaul:

_____

_____

_____

Chapters 17–19 of Book 4: bridging the Rhine:

_____

_____

_____

Chapters 13–19 of Book 6: the customs of the Gauls, including the Druids:

_____

_____

_____

Chapters 25–28 of Book 6: the animals of the Hercynian Forest:

_____

_____

_____

V. Test yourself! Label the blank map with the following:

1. Gallia Cisalpīna/Gallia Citerior (Northern Italy)

2. Gallia Transalpīna/Gallia Ulterior/ Prōvincia (Southern France)

3. Belgae (low countries)

4. Aquītanī

5. Gallia Celtica (central France)

6. Alesia

7. Lutetia (Paris)

8. Massilia (Marseilles)

9. Rōma (Rome)

10. Venetī (Brittany)

11. Aeduī

12. Sēquanī

13. Helvētiī (Swiss)

14. Nerviī

15. Arar (Saône)

16. Rhēnus (Rhine)

17. Dānuvius (Danube)

18. Sēquana (Seine)

19. Rhodanus (Rhône)

20. Mātrona (Marne)

21. Garumna (Garonne)

22. Tiberis (Tiber)

23. Rubicō (Rubicon)

24. Britannia (Britain)

25. Hispānia (Spain)

26. Germānia (Germany)

27. Pȳrēnaeī Montēs (Pyrénées)

28. Alpēs Montēs (Alps)

29. Lacus Lemanus (Lake Geneva)

30. Mare (H)Ādriāticum (Adriatic)

VI. Caesar Projects

1. Posters

- map of ancient Gaul; be sure to include a compass rose.

- a Roman foot soldier with his equipment labeled in Latin and English

- the plan of a Roman camp with labels in Latin and English

2. Find an illustration and use balsa wood or popsicle sticks to make a model of one of the following Roman war machines:

- *scorpiō*

- *ballista*

- *turris ambulātōria*

GAUL

TRANSLATION OF EXERCISE II

Respondē breviter Latīnē = Answer briefly in Latin.

1. Quis erat Vercingetorix? = Who was Vercingetorix?

2. Quot partēs habēbat Gallia? = How many parts did Gaul have?

3. Ubi Caesar pōntem magnum aedificāvit? = Where did Caesar build a big bridge?

4. Ubi sunt Alpēs Montēs? = Where are the Alps?

XI. Britannia
Roman Britain

Iūlius Caesar invaded Britannia twice, once in 55 BCE, once in 54 BCE. No lasting results came from either incursion. Instead, it was the Emperor Claudius who succeeded in making Britannia a Roman province. The Romans remained in Britain until 410 CE when the last legions were forced to withdraw.

Let's look first at the area where Caesar mounted his attacks. His initial landing was near Dūbris (Dover) on the south coast of England. He retreated because a storm damaged some of his ships. The next year, although he marched as far as the river Tamesis (Thames), he again withdrew without a clear victory because he needed to return to Gaul to deal with unrest there.

Almost one hundred years later, in 43 CE, Claudius's troops under Aulus Plautius landed near the present town of Richborough. They won a decisive battle against the Catūvellaunī, the most powerful tribe, in southern England. The Romans then established Camulodūnum (Colchester) as their center of operations. Many local chieftains allied themselves with Rome. Cogidubnus was one such early ally of Rome. In subsequent campaigns, more territory came under Roman control. One of the Romans' most famous successes was against a Druid stronghold on Mona (the Isle of Anglesey).

In 60 CE, Queen Boudicca led a revolt against the Romans. Her supporters burned Camulodūnum and Verulānium (St. Albans) near London, but the Romans soon regained control of southern England, and Boudicca was forced to commit suicide. A few years later a Roman general named Agricola led troops into Calēdonia (Scotland), and won a victory at Mōns Grauppius. He did not, however, venture into the highlands of Scotland. In 122 CE the Emperor Hadrian visited England and work began on the stone wall seventy-three miles in length that bears his name. Vallum Hadriānum (Hadrian's Wall) marked the northern border of the territory controlled by the Romans for a generation. After Hadrian's death, his successor, Antoninus Pius, established a new frontier north of Hadrian's Wall. The Vallum Antōnīnum (Antonine Wall) was a wall of turf and earth about thirty-seven miles long. It was abandoned in 180 CE.

For more than three hundred years, Roman culture dominated England. Roman roads connected towns whose inhabitants were thoroughly Romanized. Wealthy Britons copied Roman fashions. Towns like Londīnium (London), Isca (Exeter), Līndum (Lincoln), and Eborācum (York) flourished. Villas like Fishbourne and Bignor near Novīomagus (Chicester) were decorated with elegant mosaics similar to those found in other parts of the Roman Empire. Aquae Sūlis (Bath) boasted elaborate *thermae* (baths) that resembled those in Rome, and Sūlis, a local Celtic goddess of water, was associated with Minerva, the Roman goddess of war and wisdom.

EXERCISES

I. Give the modern name for each and highlight it on the map:

1. Londīnium _____

2. Verulānium _____

3. Camulodūnum _____

4. Isca _____

5. Aquae Sūlis _____

6. Novīomagus _____

7. Līndum _____

8. Eborācum _____

9. Calēdonia _____

10. Mona _____

11. Tamesis _____

II. Locate the following:

1. Hadrian's Wall

2. the Antonine Wall

3. Fishbourne Roman Villa

4. Fosse Way

III. Repondē breviter Latīnē.

1. Quid fēcit Caesar post tempestātem?

    _____

2. Quis erat Cogidubnus?

    _____

3. Ubi erant magnae thermae in Britanniā?

    _____

Roman Britain

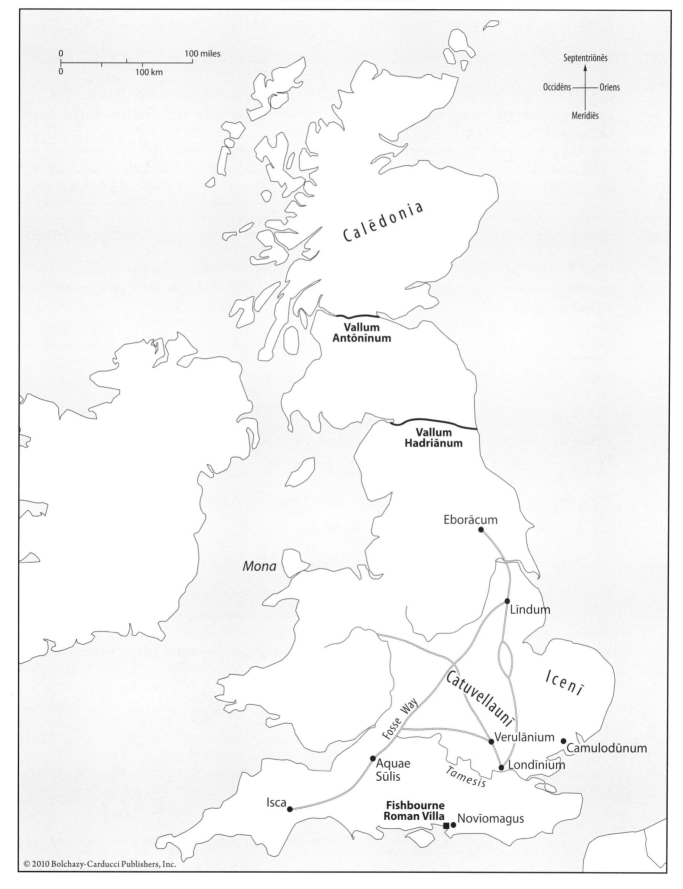

IV. Īre ulterius

1. If Eborācum is the Latin name for the city of York, how would you say "New York" in Latin?

_____

2. Read or translate Chapter 4 of Book 24 of the *Gallic Wars* in which the gallant eagle bearer of the tenth legion leads the troops when they have to disembark in deep water as Caesar launches his attack on England. Report what you have learned to your classmates.

_____

_____

_____

3. What does the Latin word *castra* mean? In English, *castra* became "chester." Find as many names as possible of towns in England that end in "chester" or "cester." Then, find some more such towns in the United States.

_____

_____

_____

4. Where was the Roman road called the Fosse Way? What does the Latin word *fossa* mean in English? Why would a *fossa* be an appropriate name for a Roman road?

_____

_____

_____

5. Grain for the troops stationed on Hadrian's Wall was brought by sea to the Tyne River north of Newcastle. It was then unloaded and stored in warehouses at an outpost called Arbeia. The sailors who manned the boats in the Tyne were called the Tigranes. They came from the eastern part of the Roman Empire, and they were especially skilled at operating in shallow water because of their experience navigating on a major river in their homeland. Name the river.

_____

ROMAN BRITAIN

V. Test yourself! Label the blank map with the following:

1. Londīnium (London)
2. Verulānium (St. Albans)
3. Camulodūnum (Colchester)
4. Isca (Exeter)
5. Aquae Sūlis (Bath)
6. Novīomagus (Chicester)
7. Līndum (Lincoln)
8. Eborācum (York)
9. Calēdonia (Scotland)
10. Mona (the Isle of Anglesey)
11. Tamesis (Thames)
12. Vallum Hadriānum (Hadrian's Wall)
13. Vallum Antōnīnum (the Antonine Wall)
14. Fishbourne Roman Villa
15. Fosse Way (Fossa = ditch)

VI. Projects for Roman Britain

1. Posters

Pick one of the following subjects and find and print pictures from Google Images. Arrange the pictures on a poster for your classroom.

- Fishbourne
- Bignor
- Aquae Sūlis
- Hadrian's Wall
- Arbeia
- Housesteads or Vindolanda

2. Short Oral Presentations

Pick one of the following subjects and find out more about it. Share the information you have found with your classmates. Be sure to give credit to your sources.

- the Roman general Agricola. Why is so much known about his life?
- the war chariots used by the Britons
- Boudicca
- Septimius Severus's campaigns in Britain
- the Mithraea found in Britain

TRANSLATION OF EXERCISE III

Respondē breviter Latīnē = Answer briefly in Latin.

1. Quid fēcit Caesar post tempestātem? = What did Caesar do after the storm?

2. Quis erat Cogidubnus? = Who was Cogidubnus?

3. Ubi erant magnae thermae in Britanniā? = Where were great baths in England?

XII. Epicī Antīquī
Ancient Epics

Two of the great epics of antiquity involve voyages. Homer's *Odyssey* is the tale of Odysseus's adventures on his journey home to Ithaca after the Trojan War. Vergil's *Aeneid*, on the other hand, tells of Aeneas's journey to a new homeland in a western land called Hesperia. It is not possible, of course, to identify all the places mentioned in an ancient work of fiction, but we can see generally what each journey entailed, and we can compare Odysseus's journey with that of Aeneas.

Let us begin by locating Trōia at the mouth of the Hellespontus (Hellespont). Remember that Sparta, the home of King Menelaus and the beautiful Helen, lies in Graecia in the Peloponnēsus. Odysseus's home was the island of Ithaca off the western coast of Graecia. Like the other Greek heroes, Odysseus was summoned by Menelaus to retrieve Helen when she had been kidnapped by Paris, Prince of Troy. The Greek fleet gathered at Aulīs before setting sail across the Mare Aegaeum. When the Greeks arrived at Trōia, they laid siege to the city. The war raged for ten years until Trōia finally fell, and Odysseus and his men were able to return to Ithaca. Modern authors and film makers have tried to identify the places Odysseus visited on his homeward journey, but only a few, like the island of the Cyclopes and the lair of Scylla and Charybdis, can be identified with certainty. Remember that the Cyclopes are associated with Hephaistos's workshop in the bowels of Aetna Mōns on the island of Sicilia. Remember also that the Fretum Sicilum, the narrow strait between Sicily and the mainland of Italy, was the home of the mythical monsters Scylla and Charybdis.

Like Odysseus, Aeneas began his journey in Trōia. While the goal of Odysseus's journey was to return home to his beloved Ithaca, wife Penelope, and son Telemachus, Aeneas was a refugee, rescued from the war by his mother Venus, to found a new Troy. Vergil tells us that after Trōia was destroyed, Aeneas went first to Thrācia. You can see Thrācia on the map northeast of Trōia on the shores of the Pontus Euxīnus. From there, guided by his father's advice, Aeneas led his band of Trojans first to Dēlos and then to Crēta. From Crēta he journeyed along the western coast of Graecia, stopping at the Strophades Islands where the Harpies, hideous female monsters, stole the Trojans' food. Another stop in western Graecia proved barren for the Trojans: in Būthrōtum, located in the area of Greece called Ēpīrus, Aeneas found other refugees from Trōia, but no resting place for his followers. King Helenus of Būthrōtum urged him to consult the Sibyl at Cūmae so Aeneas left Ēpīrus and managed to reach Sicilia. He approached the Fretum Siculum where Scylla and Charybdis lurked, but a survivor of Odysseus's visit to Sicilia warned the Trojans to avoid the Cyclops, so they turned south, away from the Fretum Siculum. They put in at the port of Drepanum just after the death of Aeneas's father. After this stay in Sicilia, Aeneas and his comrades had set sail once more for western Italy when they were blown off course by a huge storm sent by the goddess Iūno. Cast ashore in north Africa, Aeneas fell in love with Dīdō, queen of Carthāgō. Eventually, he was recalled to his duty, when Jupiter sent Mercury down to remind him of his divine mission to found a new kingdom. After a second visit to Sicilia, Aeneas brought his followers safely to the Sinus Cūmānus where he was able to consult the Sibyl at Cūmae and visit his father in the Underworld. The last of Aeneas's adventures brought him up the Tiberis where he visited Pallantēum, a city located on the very site where Rōma would one day rise.

EXERCISES

I.   Highlight on the *"Journey of Odysseus"* map:

1.   Trōia (Troy)
2.   Ithaca
3.   Sicilia (Sicily)
4.   Fretum Siculum (Strait of Messina)
5.   Ītalia (Italy)
6.   Graecia (Greece)

II.   Highlight on the *"Journey of Aeneas"* map:

1.   Trōia/Īlium (Troy)
2.   Sparta
3.   Ithaca
4.   Thrācia (Thrace)
5.   Dēlos
6.   Crēta (Crete)
7.   Strophades
8.   Būthrōtum
9.   Ācroceraunia
10.   Sicilia (Sicily)
11.   Aetna Mōns (Mt. Etna)
12.   Fretum Siculum (Strait of Messina)
13.   Drepanum
14.   Carthāgō (Carthage)
15.   Cūmae
16.   Lāvīnium

III.   Respondē breviter Latīnē.

1.   Quis Ithacae habitābat?

   _____

2.   Quis erat rēgīna Spartae? Quis erat rēx?

   _____

3.   Quis erat rēgīna Carthāginis?

   _____

4.   Ubi habitābat Sibylla?

   _____

"Journey of Odysseus"

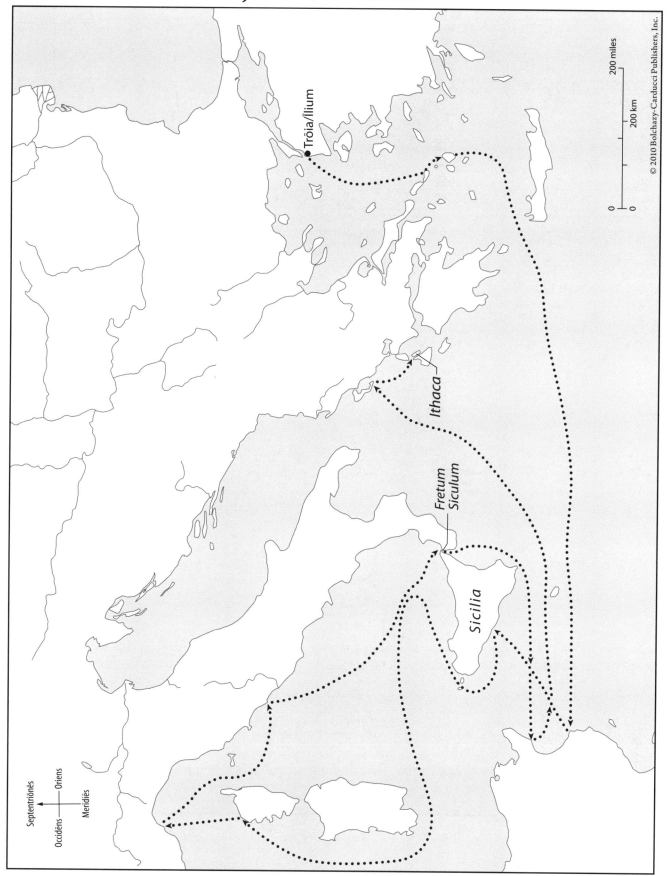

"Journey of Aeneas"

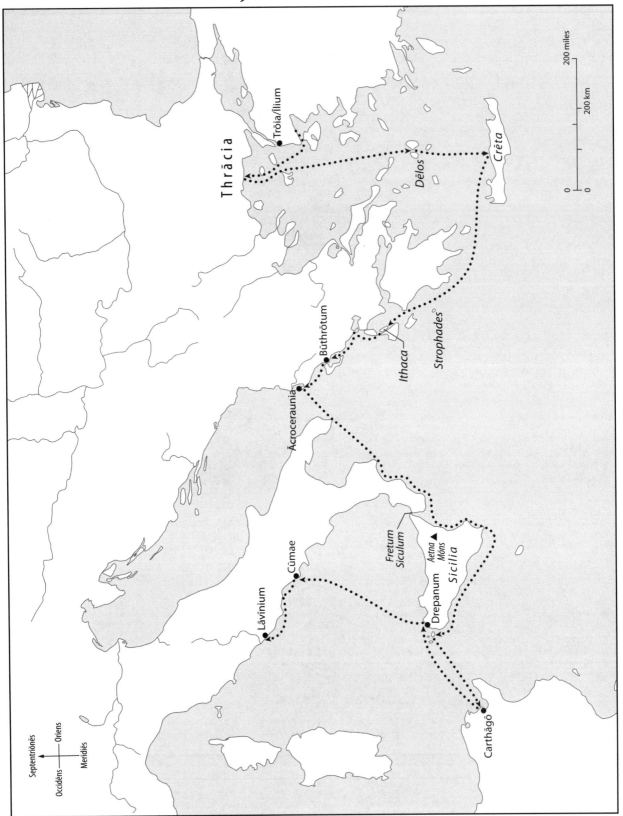

IV. Īre ulterius

1. In the *Aeneid*, Italy is sometimes called Hesperia. What is the derivation of the name Hesperia?

_____

_____

_____

2. Vergil has many different names for the Greeks, the Trojans, and the Carthaginians. List three names for each group:

_____

_____

_____

3. According to the *Aeneid*, the names of Cape Palinūrus, Cape Mīsēnum, and Cāiēta were derived from characters in the epic. Who were Palinūrus (Book 5), Mīsēnus (Book 6), and Cāiēta (Book 7)?

_____

_____

_____

4. In line 2 of Book 6 of the *Aeneid*, Vergil describes Cumae as Euboean. Where is Euboea? What is its connection with the Bay of Naples? Hint: remember what you read in chapter 6 about the settlement of this area of Italy.

_____

_____

_____

V. Epic Project

Enlarge a map of the Mediterranean and indicate by different colored lines the journeys of Odysseus and of Aeneas.

TRANSLATION OF EXERCISE III

Respondē breviter Latīnē = Answer briefly in Latin.

1. Quis Ithacae habitābat? = Who lived in Ithaca?

2. Quis erat rēgīna Spartae? Quis erat rēx? = Who was the queen of Sparta? Who was the king?

3. Quis erat rēgīna Carthāginis? = Who was the queen of Carthage?

4. Ubi habitābat Sibylla? = Where did the Sibyl live?

XIII. Scrīptōrēs Latīnī
Latin Authors

Part I: Ancient Latin Writers

When you study an ancient work of literature, it is often helpful to know a little about the author's life. It can be interesting to know where he was born and where he spent his life. Let's consider the lives of some of ancient Rome's best known writers.

Students of Roman history know **Gaius Iūlius Caesar** as a general, political leader, and revolutionary. Students of Latin also know him as the author of *Commentāriī dē bellō Gallicō* and *Commentāriī dē bellō civili*. Caesar was born and grew up in Rōma. As a young man, he was forced to flee the city for a time to avoid persecution by the dictator Sulla. Later, Caesar fought in Asia in the war against Mithradates, King of Pontus, and studied on the island of Rhodus under the orator Apollōnius Molo. In 61 BCE, Caesar served for a year as *propraetor* (governor) in Ibēria. From 58 BCE TO 49 BCE, he conducted a series of successful campaigns in Gallia. Afterward, he fought to support the claim of Cleopatra to the throne of Aegyptus in the Alexandrine War and eventually to defeat the supporters of Pompey in the Civil War. Some of Caesar's most famous victories include the Battle of Pharsālus in Graecia, the Battle of Zela in Pontus, the Battle of Thapsus in Africa, and the Battle of Munda in Hispānia.

Unlike Caesar, **Marcus Tullius Cicero** is known as an orator and essayist, not as a soldier. Cicero was born in the town of Arpīnum, sixty miles southeast of Rōma. Cicero's family moved to Rōma when he was still a child, and there, he grew up, studied oratory, and began his career as an advocate. In his late twenties, Cicero journeyed to Graecia accompanied by his brother Quintus. In Athēnae, Cicero visited his old friend Titus Pompōnius, who had made his home there. Pompōnius was so thoroughly at home in Athēnae that he was given the name Atticus, because Athens lies in the region called Attica. Atticus remained in Graecia for the rest of his life, but he and Cicero exchanged frequent letters and remained close friends.

Upon his return from Graecia, Cicero acquired a house in Rōma as well as two country villas, one at Tusculum and the other at Formiae. In the years that followed, Cicero's career took him to Sicilia, Thessalonīca, and Cilicia. During the civil war between Caesar and Pompey, Cicero supported Pompey, and after Pompey's defeat at Pharsālus, he was forced to retire to his villa in Tusculum. When his enemy Mark Antony came to power, Cicero tried to escape to Graecia. He boarded a ship, but bad weather forced it to return to shore, and he was assassinated not far from his villa at Formiae.

If you have read Cicero's *Prō Caeliō* or Catullus' Poem 49, you know that **Catullus** was Cicero's contemporary. Catullus was born near Vērōna in Gallia Cisalpīna, but he came to Rōma as a young man. Later, he was appointed to the staff of the Roman governor of Bīthȳnia. While on this assignment, he visited his brother's tomb near Trōia. After his service in Bīthȳnia, Catullus lived in Rōma although he also spent time in the villa he owned outside of Rōma. Catullus often used geographical references in his poems so you may find the maps of Graecia and Ītalia helpful when you translate his works.

Like Cicero and Catullus, the poet **Horace** was not born in Rōma. His birthplace was the small town of Venusia in Āpūlia. Like Cicero, Horace spent time in Graecia as a young man. In fact, he fought in Brutus's army at the battle of Philippī. When Augustus granted amnesty to his former enemies, the supporters of Brutus, Horace gratefully returned to Ītalia. He lived in Rōma, and *Satire* 1.9 describes an encounter with a boring acquaintance in the Forum. Another poem, *Satire* 1.5, records an uncomfortable journey Horace took from Rōma to Brundisium. We also know from Horace's *Odes* that he owned a villa in the hills outside of Rōma.

Vergil, who is the most celebrated of Latin poets, was born in a small town called Andes near Mantua in Gallia Cisalpīna. He came to Rōma as a young man, but spent most of his adult life near Neāpolis. Although he wrote vividly about the wanderings of the epic hero Aeneas, Vergil was not a great traveler himself. In fact, one of his rare journeys was a visit to Graecia in 19 BCE. It was on this trip that he became fatally ill. He returned to Ītalia but died in Brundisium and was buried in Neāpolis.

Ovid, the author of the *Metamorphōsēs*, was born in the mountain town of Sulmo in what is today the Abruzzo. Ovid's father moved the family to Rōma when Ovid was still a child. Ovid spent time in his youth in Athēnae. He also visited Trōia. He then lived in Rōma until he was involved in a scandal and exiled to Tomi, a town on the Pontus Euxīnus near the mouth of the Dānuvius. Here, Ovid spent the last years of his life and died still hoping to be recalled to Rōma.

Of course, Catullus, Horace, Vergil, and Ovid are far from the only Latin poets of note. **Tibullus** and **Propertius** are celebrated for their elegiac poetry; **Juvenal** and **Martial** are known for their stinging satire. Not one of these writers was born in the city of Rōma although each spent a large part of his life there. Tibullus was probably born at Pedum, a small town near Tibur (Tivoli) while Propertius was born in Umbria north of Rōma, perhaps in Asisium (Assisi). Juvenal was born in Aquīnum, which is not far from Rōma in the region of Latium. Martial was actually born in Bilbilis, in Hispānia, not far from the modern town of Zaragosa.

In addition to her poets, Rōma can boast of two great writers of comedy, **Plautus** and **Terence**. Plautus's birthplace is thought to be Sarsina, a small town in Umbria in northern Italy. Terrence, on the other hand, was born in Carthāgō. He was sold into slavery and brought to Rōma where his master eventually freed him.

Other well known Latin writers include the historians **Sallust**, **Livy**, **Suetonius**, and **Tacitus**. Notice once again that none of these authors claimed Rome as his birthplace. Sallust, for example, was born in Amiternum, a town sixty miles northeast of Rōma. Sallust wrote about the Catilinarian conspiracy and about the war with Jugurtha, a North African king. Livy, whose great work *Ab Urbe Conditā* tells of the early history of Rome, was born in Patavium (Padua) in Gallia Cisalpīna. Suetonius's birthplace was a North African town called Hippō Rēgius in what is now Algeria, while Tacitus was probably born in Vasio, a town in Gallia Transalpīna.

Additional ancient writers of prose include a biographer, a scientist, and a letter writer. You may know that Catullus dedicated his book of poems to a man called Cornelius. This was **Cornelius Nepos**, a writer of biography. Nepos also wrote a history entitled *Chronica,* but the manuscript of this work has been lost. Like Catullus, Nepos was born near Vērōna in Gallia Cisalpīna. **Pliny the Elder** was yet another native of Gallia Cisalpīna. You may remember that Pliny the Elder was the admiral in charge of the Roman fleet on the Bay of Naples at the time of the eruption of Vesuvius Mōns and that he actually died trying to rescue victims of the eruption. Pliny was also a man of science whose *Hīstoria Nātūrālis* was read for hundreds of years. He was born in the town of Cōmum, and so was his nephew and adopted son, known as **Pliny the Younger**. The younger Pliny was the author of numerous letters on various topics, including the two letters with his eyewitness account of the eruption of Vesuvius, written at the request of the historian Tacitus.

EXERCISES

I.   Give the birthplace of each author. Then highlight each birthplace on the map.

1. Caesar _____

2. Cicero _____

3. Catullus _____

4. Horace _____

5. Vergil _____

6. Ovid _____

7. Tibullus _____

8. Propertius _____

9. Juvenal _____

10. Martial _____

11. Plautus _____

12. Terence _____

13. Sallust _____

14. Livy _____

15. Tacitus _____

16. Suetonius _____

17. Cornelius Nepos _____

18. Pliny the Elder _____

19. Pliny the Younger _____

ANCIENT LATIN WRITERS

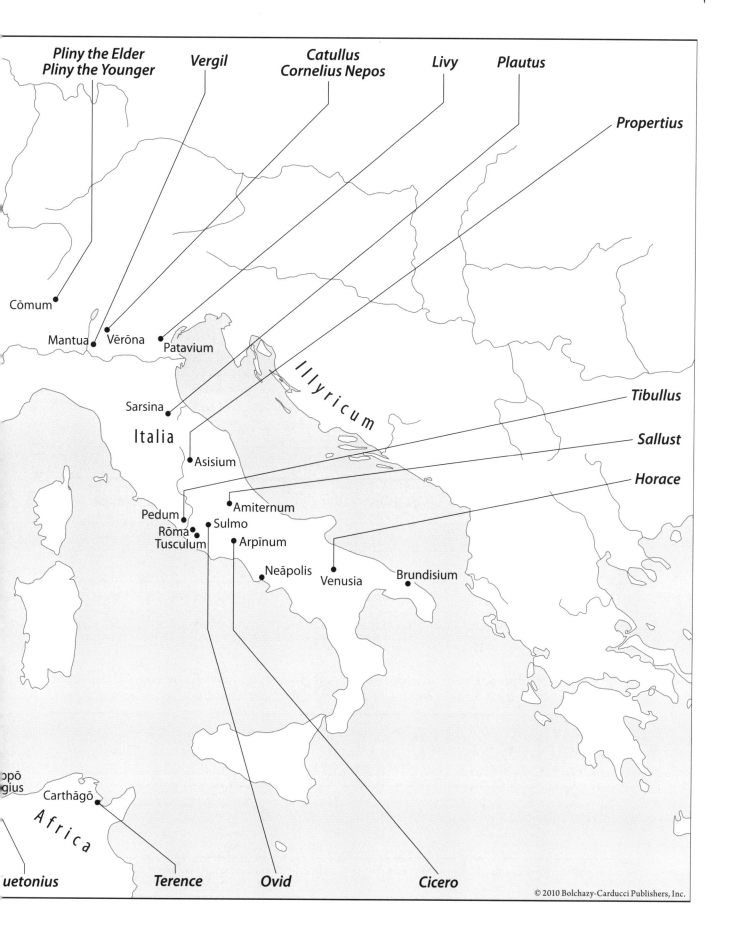

Pliny the Elder
Pliny the Younger

Vergil

Catullus
Cornelius Nepos

Livy

Plautus

Propertius

Cōmum

Mantua · Vērōna
Patavium

I l l y r i c u m

Sarsina

Tibullus

Italia

Sallust

Asisium

Horace

Amiternum

Pedum
Rōma
Tusculum

Sulmo

Arpīnum

Neāpolis

Venusia

Brundisium

opō
gius

Carthāgō

Africa

uetonius

Terence

Ovid

Cicero

II. List the following.

    1. one (1) biographer:

    _____

    2. one (1) letter writer:

    _____

    3. one (1) scientist:

    _____

    4. two (2) satirists:

    _____

    5. two (2) writers of comedy:

    _____

    6. five (5) historians:

    _____

    _____

    7. five (5) poets:

    _____

    _____

III. Cōgitā dē nōminibus oppidōrum, urbium, īnsulārum parvārumque in grammaticā Latīnā. Tum respondē breviter Latīnē.

    1. Ubi Cicero natus est?

    _____

    2. Ubi Vergilius natus est?

    _____

    3. Ubi Ovidius mortuus est?

    _____

IV. Īre ulterius

1. Find information about Caesar's most important victories: Alesia, Pharsālus, Zela, Thapsus, and Munda. Give the name of Caesar's opponent along with the date and location of each:

_____

_____

_____

_____

_____

2. Why did Cicero's *Philippics* inflame Mark Antony's enmity toward Cicero? Why are these orations called *Philippics*?

_____

_____

_____

3. Explain the opening line of the inscription on Vergil's tomb: "Mantua mē genuit; Calabri rapuēre; tenet nunc Parthenope . . ."

_____

_____

_____

4. How far from Rome was each author's birthplace?

Cicero: Arpīnum = ? miles from Rome _____

Catullus: Verōna = ? miles from Rome _____

Horace: Venusia in Āpūlia = ? miles from Rome _____

Vergil: Andes near Mantua = ? miles from Rome _____

Ovid: Sulmo = ? miles from Rome _____

TRANSLATION OF EXERCISE III

Cogitā dē nōminibus oppidōrum, urbium, īnsulārum parvārumque in grammaticā Latīnā. Tum respondē breviter Latīnē = Think about the names of towns, cities, and small islands in Latin grammar. Then answer briefly in Latin.

1. Ubi Cicero natus est? = Where was Cicero born?

2. Ubi Vergilius natus est? = Where was Vergil born?

3. Ubi Ovidius mortuus est? = Where did Ovid die?

Part II: Later Writers of Latin

The barbarian invasions of Italy coupled with a sharp decline in the population spelled the end of Rome's domination of Western Europe. But even as Rome fell, Latin remained alive. It served as the common language of all educated people in Western Europe for hundreds of years. Churchmen like the Venerable Bede, historians like William of Tyre, poets like Petrarch, and scientists like Copernicus, Galileo, and Kepler all wrote in Latin.

Let's turn to the map of Europe and note some of the places identified with famous writers of late Latin. For example, the **Venerable Bede**, a Benedictine monk, lived and wrote near Newcastle on Tyne in northern England in the late seventh century and early eighth century. Bede's most famous work is his *Historia ecclēsiastica gentis Anglōrum*, ("The Ecclesiastical History of the English People"). He is called "the Venerable" because he was greatly revered by later writers.

Einhard, who served the Holy Roman emperor Charlemagne at his court in Aachen, Germany, was a contemporary of the Venerable Bede. Although he came from a humble background, Einhard was educated at a monastic school where he had studied Latin grammar and literature. He was attracted to Charlemagne's court, where administrators fluent in Latin were welcome because Latin was the official language of Charlemagne's empire. Einhard is best known for the biography he wrote of Charlemagne, *Vita Carolī Magnī* (The Life of Charlemagne").

Peter Abelard was born in Brittany in 1079. Brittany is a rugged peninsula in northwest France that juts into the English Channel south of Normandy. Abelard went to Paris as a young man; there he became a respected teacher and theologian. Unfortunately, Abelard fell in love with Heloise, a young woman whom he was tutoring. Abelard tells the story of their star-crossed love in his autobiography, *Historia calamitātum meārum* ("The Story of My Sufferings"). The letters of Abelard and Heloise written in Latin can still be read.

William of Tyre is the author of a history of the Crusades in Latin called *Historia rērum in partibus trānsmarīnīs gestārum.* ("The Narrative of Deeds Done in Regions across the Sea"). He came from a family that had taken part in the earliest crusades. He was born in Jerusalem, but spent much of his adult life in Tyre where he served as archbishop. He died in Tyre in 1185.

Petrarch, one of the best-known scholars and authors of the early Renaissance, was born near Florence in 1304. He spent much of his life in Avignon in southern France, where the papal court was located from 1307–1377. Petrarch wrote his famous sonnets in Italian, but many of his other works such as *Africa,* an unfinished epic about Hannibal, and *Dē virīs illūstribus*, a series of biographies, are in Latin. Petrarch was so steeped in the works of ancient authors that he once wrote a letter addressed to Cicero, who had been dead for more than a thousand years!

Lorenzo Valla was born almost a century after Petrarch, but like his learned predecessors, Valla wrote and lectured in Latin. In fact, Valla was very interested in Latin grammar and is known for his essay, *Ēlegantiārum linguae Latīnae librī sex* ("Six Books of Proper Uses of the Latin Language"). He lived much of his life in Naples, where he served as secretary to the court of Alfonso of Aragon.

The famous Renaissance writer **Erasmus** was born in Rotterdam ca. 1466 but travelled widely throughout his life. He was ordained as a priest, but he criticized the Catholic clergy in his satire *Stultitiae Laus* ("In Praise of Folly"). A dedicated and gifted scholar, he prepared a new Latin translation of the New Testament based on a close reading of the Greek manuscripts. This task took him to Basel where he worked closely with his publisher. A list of his correspondents is a "who's who" of his day.

Thomas More was an English contemporary and friend of Erasmus. More served King Henry VIII as a diplomat and later as Chancellor, but he is probably best known as the author of *Ūtopia*, a treatise in Latin that describes an ideal state. More opposed Henry VIII's divorce from Katherine of Aragon and Henry's asserting supremacy over the church. He retired to his home outside of London but soon was imprisoned in the Tower of London. He was finally beheaded in 1535.

Have you ever wondered how historians today learn about the early exploration of the New World by European explorers like Christopher Columbus? In fact, much of the information scholars still rely on comes from the work of **Petrus Martyr**, who was born in Italy in 1457. He was the chaplain at the court of King Ferdinand and Queen Isabella in Barcelona, Spain. In this capacity he had access to Columbus's letters and was also able to interview later explorers. Although he never visited the New World himself, his *Dē orbe novō* ("Concerning the New World") is a useful resource for historians.

Juan Sepúlveda, was born in 1494. Like Petrus Martyr, Sepúlveda served the king of Spain at the court in Barcelona. Sepúlveda was a theologian and scholar who translated several of Aristotle's works into Latin. He is known for arguing that Spain had the right to colonize the New World and that the native inhabitants of the newly discovered lands should be treated like children!

Sepúlveda and Petrus Martyr wrote about the New World, but in the sixteenth century people in western Europe were interested in the Orient as well as the Americas. Born in 1536, **Petreus Maffeius** was a Jesuit who lived in Lisbon, Portugal, and wrote about Jesuit missionaries in distant places, including China and Japan. His *Historiae Indicae* ("History of India") became enormously popular because people were eager to learn about the faraway lands he described. All of Maffeius' works are in Latin because Latin continued to be the language of educated people in all parts of western Europe.

Scientists especially relied on Latin when they wanted to publish their findings or discuss their discoveries with colleagues. For example, **Nicolaus Copernicus**, an astronomer who was educated at the University of Krakow in Poland, wrote his famous treatise *Dē revolūtiōnibus orbium caelestium* ("About the Revolutions of the Celestial Bodies") in Latin. This work set forth Copernicus's landmark theory that the earth is not the center of the universe but instead revolves around the sun. Seventy years later, in 1610, the Italian astronomer **Galileo Galilei** was the object of persecution because he promoted Copernicus's theory. Galileo, who had taught at both the University of Pisa and at the University of Padua, was summoned to Rome twice for questioning. He was convicted of heresy in 1633 and required to live in seclusion, first in Siena, later in the small town of Arcetri where he died in 1642. Ironically, these years of house arrest were some of his most productive.

Like Copernicus and Galileo, **Johannes Kepler** was a renowned astronomer who wrote in Latin. As a young man, Kepler taught mathematics and astronomy in Graz, Austria. Here, in 1594 at age 23, he published *Mystērium Cosmographicum* ("The Cosmographic Mystery") defending Copernicus's theory. Later, Kepler moved to Prague, where he wrote *Astronomia Nova* ("New Astronomy"), which defined the laws of planetary motion. In addition to these serious scientific works, Kepler also wrote a work of fantasy called *Somnium* ("The Dream"), which involves space travel.

Copernicus, Galileo, and Kepler were all highly educated. They wrote in Latin as a matter of course. It is, therefore, surprising to see that a number of important discoveries in microbiology were made in the seventeenth century by a Dutch lens crafter named **Antōnius dē Leeuwenhoek** who knew no Latin. Leeuwenhoek, a native of Delft, was an expert at making powerful magnifying glasses. He used the lenses to examine muscle fibers, blood flowing in capillaries, and his own saliva. He was fascinated by the animalcules or microorganisms that were invisible without the use of his lenses. Because he did not know Latin, Leeuwenhoek wrote letters about his discoveries in Dutch to the Royal Society of London, and one of the society's members translated the letters into Latin!

As we have seen, Latin was the language of educated people for hundreds of years, whether they lived in England like the Venerable Bede or in Poland like Copernicus. It is perhaps fitting that we should conclude this discussion with the man who is considered the "Father of Danish Literature," **Ludvig Holberg**. Born in Copenhagen in 1684, Holberg became a professor at the University of Copenhagen. He wrote comedies and satires in Danish, but one of his best known works is in Latin: *Iter subterrāneum* ("The Underground Journey"). The hero of the story is a young man who finds his way underground to a land full of talking trees!

Exercises

I. Give the name of the city most closely associated with each of the following writers:

1. Bede   _____

2. Einhard   _____

3. Abelard   _____

4. William of Tyre   _____

5. Petrarch   _____

6. Valla   _____

7. Erasmus   _____

8. Thomas More   _____

9. Petrus Martyr   _____

10. Sepúlveda   _____

11. Maffeius   _____

12. Copernicus   _____

13. Kepler   _____

14. Leeuwenhoek   _____

15. Holberg   _____

II. Highlight the cities associated with each of the authors in I above.

III. Translate each title and give the author of each work:

1. _Vita Carolī Magnī_

    _____

2. _Historia ecclēsiastica gentis Anglōrum_

    _____

3. _Stultitiae Laus_

    _____

Later Latin Writers

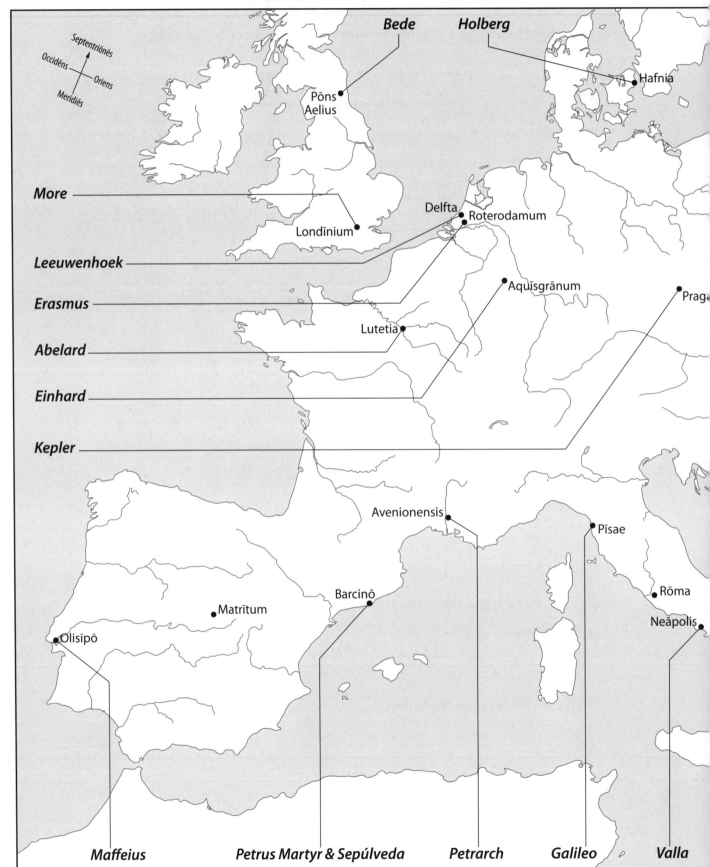

Copernicus

© 2010 Bolchazy-Carducci Publishers, Inc.

0 _____ 300 miles
0 _____ 300 km

Cracōvia

Pontus Euxīnus

Constantīnoplis/
Istanbul

Athēnae

Mare Internum

Hierosolyma

William of Tyre

4. *Historia calamitātum meārum*

_____

5. *Dē orbe novō*

_____

6. *Ūtopia*

_____

7. *Somnium*

_____

8. *Historiae Indicae*

_____

9. *Astronomia Nova*

_____

10. *Iter subterrāneum*

_____

IV. Respondē breviter Latīnē.

1. Quis est auctor *Africae*?

_____

2. Quem Heloīsa amāvit?

_____

3. In fābulā, *Iter subterrāneum* nomine, quid faciunt arborēs?

_____

V.   Īre ulterius

1.   Why did Petrarch address Cicero as "Tully"?

2.   Find out the origin of Erasmus's name. What is the Greek word from which "Erasmus" comes? What were his other two names? Explain why Erasmus chose each of the names.

3.   Some people teased Erasmus by saying that he was a *mūs errāns*. What does the phrase mean and why did it fit Erasmus?

4.   What is an homunculus? Where did Leeuwenhoek say he saw one?

5.   What kind of education did Thomas More give his daughters? Which daughter followed most closely in her father's footsteps as a scholar?

6.   What is Galileo supposed to have said at the end of his trial after he had been convicted? What did he mean?

TRANSLATION OF EXERCISE IV

Respondē breviter Latīnē = Answer briefly in Latin.

1. Quis est auctor *Africae*? = Who was the author of *Africa*?

2. Quem Heloïsa amāvit? = Whom did Eloise love?

3. In fābulā, *Iter subterrāneum* nomine, quid faciunt arborēs? = In the story, *The Underground Journey* by name, what do the trees do?

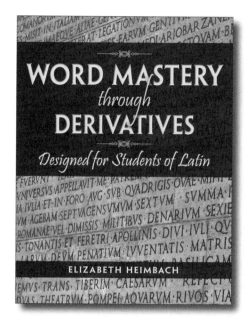

Word Mastery through Derivatives
Designed for Students of Latin

Elizabeth Heimbach

Student Text: viii + 163 pp. (2017) 8½" x 11" Paperback
ISBN 978-0-86516-853-4

Teacher's Guide: x + 393 pp. (2017) 8½" x 11" Spiral-bound
ISBN 978-0-86516-854-1

This workbook is specifically constructed for students studying Latin. Veteran teacher Elizabeth Heimbach organizes English derivatives by topic—two chapters devoted to affixes, twelve chapters presenting special topics like mythology, and eleven chapters featuring grammar-related derivatives like prepositions and deponent verb derivatives. A student-friendly and engaging narrative presents derivatives and demonstrates the symbiotic relationship between Latin and English. The text provides students the skills and practice to apply word-building analysis to their study of both Latin vocabulary and English derivatives.

Features

- twenty-five chapters organized by topic
- five to eight exercises per chapter
- "just for fun" activities for each special topic chapter
- appendices: list of derivatives broken out by chapter and a list of phrases used in English

The **Teacher's Manual** that master teacher Elizabeth Heimbach has developed is an indispensable resource for the busy novice or veteran Latin teacher. She provides comprehensive answers to all the questions in the student workbook. Recognizing that practice is key to mastery, the Teacher's Manual includes two quizzes for each chapter. To assist teachers who need to track student learning, three sets of diagnostic and post-study tests help document student progress.

Bolchazy-Carducci Publishers, Inc.
www.BOLCHAZY.com

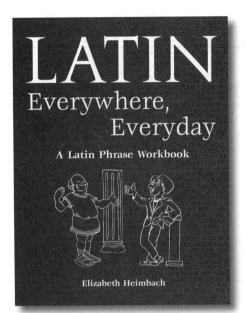

Latin Everywhere, Everyday
A Latin Phrase Workbook

Elizabeth Heimbach

Student Text: viii + 152 pp. (2004) 8½" x 11" Paperback
ISBN 978-0-86516-572-4

Teacher's Manual: iv + 164 pp. with CD (2005) 8½" x 11" Paperback
ISBN 978-0-86516-589-2

Latin Everywhere, Everyday: A Latin Phrase Workbook overflows with what students need:

- one Latin phrase for every day of the school year with five on a page so that a week's work can be viewed at one time

- a reservoir of explanations, examples, translations, and accompanying exercises

- an abundance of derivatives

- a profusion of Latin abbreviations and mottoes

- a steady stream of projects and games to engage the students in their learning

- a bubbling source of historical facts and of the ubiquity of Latin in our everyday lives

The student workbook, *Latin Everywhere, Everyday*, is designed for students who want to learn Latin phrases, abbreviations, and mottoes and how to use them correctly in English. This practical volume can also serve as an effective introduction to Latin.

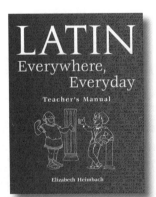

Latin Everywhere, Everyday: Teacher's Manual
The teacher's manual contains the answers to all the exercises in the student workbook along with additional exercises and answers for those who have studied Latin. Additional games and projects are also included in the teacher's manual.

The accompanying CD features James Chochola providing clear Latin pronunciation of each phrase, motto, and abbreviation.

Bolchazy-Carducci Publishers, Inc.
www.BOLCHAZY.com

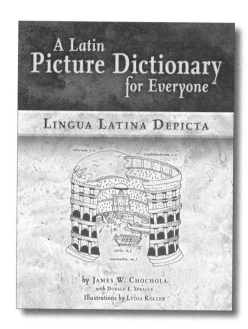

A Latin Picture Dictionary for Everyone
Lingua Latina Depicta

James Chochola
with Donald E. Sprague
Illustrations by Lydia Koller

Student Text: viii + 205 pp. (2017) 8½" x 11" Paperback
ISBN 978-0-86516-749-0

Teacher's Guide: (2017) 8½" x 11" Paperback
ISBN 978-0-86516-855-8

Everyone can learn some Latin visually!

Designed for Latin students, *A Latin Picture Dictionary for Everyone* asks the learner to make a ready connection between an image and its corresponding Latin word. Illustrated exercises provide an opportunity for students to practice with and internalize the Latin vocabulary.

Features

- Black-and-white line drawings present everyday objects and scenes from everyday life—animals and numbers, colors, the family, buildings, transportation, the house, furniture, pastimes, professions, the military, parts of the body, clothing, food shopping, food preparation, and the arts—one image from the Roman world and a corresponding image from the modern world. The line drawings invite students to color the pictures.

- Each object is drawn for ready recognition and easy connection to its Latin label.

- A set of exercises, of varied complexity, accompanies each set of illustrations.

- Appendices include Pronunciation of Classical Latin, Major Parts of Speech and Their Uses, How Latin Words Work: Nouns, Verbs, Adjectives, A Grammatical Outline

- A Pictorial Glossary of Additional Latin Vocabulary and Synonyms

Bolchazy-Carducci Publishers, Inc.
www.BOLCHAZY.com

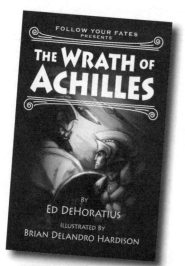

Follow Your Fates
SERIES

Ed DeHoratius's three dramatic action adventures let YOU experience firsthand the wrenching decisions of the ancient Mediterranean world's most illustrious heroes.

In *The Wrath of Achilles*, you are Achilles, the greatest hero of ancient Greece. On Troy's battlefields will you honor your code and not fight, or stand beside your men?

x + 62 pp. (2009) 5" x 7¾" Paperback, ISBN 978-0-86516-708-7

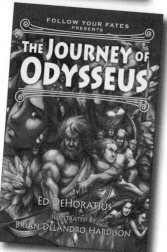

In *The Journey of Odysseus*, you are Odysseus, the wiliest hero of ancient Greece. Your love of family is as strong as your quest for adventure. What will you do, when given the choice of immortality, or when trapped in a cave by a man-eating monster?

x + 118 pp. (2009) 5" x 7¾" Paperback, ISBN 978-0-86516-710-0

In *The Exile of Aeneas*, you are Aeneas, Troy's preeminent hero. Your integrity is legendary, but can it withstand your city's destruction, grueling exile, and another war?

x + 114 pp. (2010) 5" x 7¾" Paperback, ISBN 978-0-86516-709-4

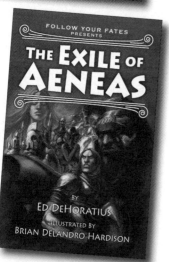

Features of each *Follow Your Fates* adventure:

- Prose story that thrusts you the reader (age 8 and up) right into the action
- Multiple different endings—depending on your choices
- Illustrations by award-winning comic book artist Brian Delandro Hardison
- Glossary of names, with pronunciation guide
- Series website: www.bolchazy.com/followyourfates

Bolchazy-Carducci Publishers, Inc.
www.BOLCHAZY.com